Among Equals: A Memoir

D1570135

Among Equals:
A Memoir

*The Rise of IBM's First
Woman Corporate Vice President*

Ruth Leach Amonette

Creative Arts Book Company
Berkeley • 1999

Among Equals is published by Donald S. Ellis
and distributed by Creative Arts Book Company

For information contact:
Creative Arts Book Company
833 Bancroft Way
Berkeley, California 94710
(800) 848-7789

ISBN 088739-218-0 Paperback
ISBN 088739-219-9 Hardcover
Library of Congress Catalog Number 98-89652

Printed in the United States of America

To my wonderful husband K Amonette,
for his patience
and for his dedication to my project

Acknowledgements

Writing a book is a process, and no one ever makes it through that journey alone. I would like to thank all those who helped me on my expedition.

First, much appreciation to my mother, who secretly collected all the letters I wrote home from 1938 to 1955. These formed the basis of my memoir. Carolyn Crippen of New York City literally taught me how to write a sentence and helped me organize my material for writing this memoir. Vicki Gibbs introduced me to the publishing world and wrote the book proposal that was sent around the country to various publishers. She has been my writer and collaborator, working with my publisher in the selection of photographs to be used in this book. Her contributions have been invaluable.

I also want to thank Jeanne Cotten Blum and Jane Haislip Creel, who lived through the IBM years with me and whose memories of those years added much to this book. Thanks also to my close assistant, Mary Schultz O'Connor. Anne Elizabeth Haislip, along with other IBMers, collected several stories for my use; Betty Hoch Frank sent her memoir for my perusal; Frances Young McCarthy also sent her IBM story to me; and Carolyn Shuck, a former IBMer, sent reams of suggestions and ideas for the book. Thanks also to Bryce Ainslee, Miss Stanford, and Erin Morita.Thanks to all others too numerous to mention who helped in many different ways. I used Tom Watson's book *Father, Son, and Company* as a reference guide to stimulate my memory of people and events from so many years ago.

A special thanks to my publisher, Don Ellis, who showed such enthusiasm for this book, and to my family for their support.

And particularly to my sister, Helen, who lived with us and taught me how to appreciate life again after I went blind.

TABLE OF CONTENTS

Among Equals: A Memoir

Preface

The IBM culture had already become deeply rooted over some 25 years when I joined the company in November 1938. As part of my job training, I learned the IBM basic beliefs formulated by Mr. Thomas J. Watson Sr. back in 1914.

The moral principle upon which he drew was the Golden Rule. However, he gave that rule a concrete application to business in what he called the three benefits. Business, he said, must benefit the customer, the stockholder, and the employee. Transactions that do not benefit all parties in the long run benefit no one. Mr. Watson also was deeply interested in IBM's personnel program, which he called human relations. He believed all human relations should be governed by the Golden Rule.

In the 1940s, it became my responsibility to pass those beliefs on to all the new IBM sales employees, many of them in the systems service department. Most systems service employees were women whom IBM had recruited to replace the hundreds of men off serving their country in World War II.

I also became a spokesperson for the IBM way of doing business in some of the speeches I gave throughout the war.

Before that time, opportunities for women in the corporate world—other than secretarial—were rare. Without the changes World War II created in the workforce and without the vision and foresight of Mr. Watson Sr., I never would have penetrated the man's world at the top of corporate life, rising in four years from a typewriter demonstrator at the World's Fair to become one of five corporate vice presidents at IBM in 1943. My experiences in IBM and the people I met along the way produced a rich tapestry of relationships, which I have treasured all these years.

I wrote this book, in part, as a tribute to all of IBM's systems service women who worked so hard during the war years to maintain and protect the revenue of the business while three-quarters of IBM's male sales force served in the armed forces or other war work.

The war provided great opportunities for women in the business world, especially at IBM, where the systems service women helped break down the barriers the country had against accepting women as peers in the workplace. And the same goes for the women in IBM factories all over the country, who operated the complicated machinery as well as any man.

Not long ago, I discovered a box of some 700 letters my mother had saved without my knowledge, letters I had written to my family from the time I left home in November 1939 to go east to work for IBM. Memories came rolling back — of long wartime meetings in Mr. Watson Sr.'s office to determine the direction of the business, long wartime train trips to keep physically in touch with field offices, acts of kindness, and moments of hilarity. I could hardly believe that I had done so much.

When they heard of this cache, two of my dearest friends and former IBMers, Jane Haislip Creel and Jeanne Cotten Blum, prevailed upon me to write about our years with IBM. Each could easily write her own memoirs, but this is my version.

We thought of ourselves as the foremothers of IBM's golden years, when Tom Watson Jr., following in his father's footsteps, built up the business and expanded the company's horizons during the decades right after the war. Wall Street and the media called IBM "Big Blue."

Today's IBM, or "New Blue," as they now call themselves, is, of necessity, an entirely different company than the one we knew. In a world of change, we all must evolve if we're to endure. But I think the basic IBM values of service, integrity and innovation still provide a strong foundation for the company to build on and thrive.

—Ruth Leach Amonette

CHAPTER ONE

Looking Back from the Peak

Feeling almost paralyzed with excitement, my parents and I hurried into the grand ballroom at the Mayflower Hotel in Washington, D.C. On that chilly evening, February 9, 1946, five hundred selected guests including President Harry Truman, members of his cabinet, plus assorted dignitaries and foreign diplomats, had assembled to honor the eleven recipients of that year's Women's National Press Club achievement awards...and I was one of the women being honored!

The list of honorees included well-known women such as choreographer Agnes de Mille and artist Georgia O'Keeffe, German physicist Lise Meitner, who helped develop the atomic bomb, and Dean Virginia Gildersleeve, president of Barnard College and United States representative to the United Nations, plus an impressive array of others, all highly successful in their chosen fields.

We sat at the head table with President Truman and several members of his cabinet. Invitations to this event were difficult to come by. My parents sat at a table with Secretary of State Jimmy Byrnes, but my boss, Mr. Thomas J. Watson Sr., founder and president of IBM and the man responsible for my being there, could not get a table for himself and his executives.

As I settled into my designated spot on the dais, my seatmate, Secretary of Labor, the Honorable L.B. Schwellenbach, turned to me and asked, "Are you somebody's secretary?"

At twenty-nine years old, I must have looked like a kid to him compared with my fellow honorees, all of whom were a great deal older. I glared at him and merely nodded my head, too annoyed to answer. He didn't deserve a response anyway.

Turning his back on this taciturn "hireling" he began chatting with the lady on his left and never said another word to me until after the president presented my award and told the audience what I had achieved during the war years. Then Mr. Schwellenbach wanted my undivided attention…he didn't get it. In spite of that incident, I had an unforgettable evening. I felt so proud to be included with that group of amazing women, and what a thrill, dining at the same table as the president of the United States…even though it was a very long table. As I sat there thinking back over the previous five years, I could hardly believe the opportunities I had been given and what I had accomplished, especially considering I had never planned to have a career in the first place.

From Old Blue (U.C. Berkeley) to Big Blue

Like most young women of that time, I never thought to prepare myself for a future career or even explore the few professional opportunities available to women. I assumed I would fall in love, marry, and start a family, which is what my sister and most of my friends did in those days. But in spite of going on plenty of dates, I never found anyone I cared deeply enough for to make a commitment.

Born in Oakland, California, I later moved with my family to nearby Piedmont, which had better schools. My parents raised my sister Helen and me in a firm fashion. Expected to conform to their strict, old-fashioned morality and work ethic, we were taught the importance of good manners, and told what words like commitment, loyalty, and integrity meant.

The stock market crash of 1929 deeply affected my parents, as it did most of their friends. But at least we were all in the same boat and could give each other moral support. If nothing else, we all learned the value of a dollar.

The Depression days proved gruesome for some of our family's friends who took pay cuts or were carried by their respective banks, as my father was, or lost their jobs completely. We spent very little money and managed to get by without any financial disaster. My family saved what they could for our education, grateful that my sister was two and a half years older so our college expenses overlapped by only two years.

There was no question that Helen and I would go to the University of California at Berkeley, where the tuition was only $26 a semester.

"Think of it, girls," said my father, "a whole year of education from one of the top universities in the country for only $52." Helen entered Berkeley in 1931 and I followed in 1933.

In those days, my social life centered around sports, partly because they were free. I played a lot of tennis, mostly with boys my age, as I liked a hard-hitting game. Summers, Helen and I spent as counselors at a Camp Fire Girls camp near Nevada City, California, where we performed all kinds of duties. As the only two certified lifeguards on the lakefront, we taught swimming as well as canoeing. We also had the honor of being the only two permitted to drive the "Big Green Truck" for as many as twenty campers on overnight trips in the Sierras. The job meant hard work and a lot of responsibility, but I enjoyed the outdoors and working with the children.

I loved those summers at camp, immersed in nature and honing our survival skills in a semi-wild forest. As a counselor-in-charge on overnight trips, I carried a hatchet for chopping up firewood or in case we encountered a mountain lion or some other wild animal—though I hated to think how I'd ever use a hatchet against a pouncing mountain lion. Maneuvering that big green truck around those mountain roads and dried up riverbeds, I felt very important and grown up at seventeen. My self-assurance improved each summer I spent at the camp.

In 1933, as my parents were barely emerging from the Depression, I entered Cal (U.C. Berkeley). No one had any money, and jobs were still scarce, but at least prices were commensurately low. Hamburgers cost a dime, beer 10 cents a glass, and movies a quarter.

Like my sister before me, I joined a sorority, but a different one from hers. I didn't want to be a "legacy" or "Helen's little sister, Ruth." The time had come for me to stand on my own two feet. Nevertheless, she and I both enjoyed the fraternal social life of those days, which consisted mostly of picnics with hot dogs, beer, Bing Crosby and big band records, and a lot of off-key singing.

By my junior year, Helen had graduated and become engaged to be married. I fell heir to her Model A Ford so I could drive to college and continue living at home. My Ford made me a popular guest at picnics, provided I drove. We also loved to form a caravan of cars for weekend gatherings around the Bay area.

At Cal I played lots of intramural tennis, the only tennis available for women to play then, and I won my '37 "numerals" in that sport.

Everything interested me and I took all kinds of courses—from anthropology to architecture and art, lots of history and lots of political science, not to mention the required courses in English, philosophy, geology, and others. There wasn't enough time for all the courses I wanted to take.

Unfortunately, by my senior year I knew I should have had better direction from my faculty advisor. I'd spread myself too thin, but by then it was too late to make up the credits. I graduated in 1937 with a bachelors degree in political science.

The summer following graduation I spent developing my tennis game, counseling at camp again, and having fun swimming, aquaplaning, picnicking and sunbathing at Lake Tahoe with my friends. My parents fondly tolerated my fling, but as summer drew to a close, my sensible father approached me early one evening to talk about Life.

"Ruthie," he said, "if you have no urgent plans to get a real job, I strongly advise you to look into a course or two at Merritt Business College in Oakland. You really should prepare yourself for the day when you have to earn your own living." He must have feared I'd be on his hands for the rest of his life. Nonetheless, my little $25 a month job at the Piedmont Camp Fire Girls office was nearing an end, so I followed his advice and enrolled at Merritt.

In those days, business college meant secretarial school. I wasn't too thrilled by the prospect of being somebody's secretary, trapped behind a desk all day, but I said I would give it a try. My best subject at Merritt was typing, which I had learned in high school and then spent four years perfecting in college, typing term papers for myself, and my friends. But shorthand became my downfall.

After a month, I fearfully approached my father and confessed. "Daddy, I simply can't write that fast. If that's how I have to earn my living, I'll probably starve. I've just got to look around for something else to do."

He felt disappointed but said, "All right, Ruthie, but keep at it, anyway, until you find something you'd like to try."

That evening in the *Oakland Tribune* I found an ad that read, "Dr. Robert Thayer, dental surgeon in Oakland, looking for a bright young lady to train as dental assistant. Please apply, etc." The job sounded professional and intrigued me, and I was thrilled when the dentist hired me. But the excitement quickly died when I saw how grotesque the work really was. The doctor wanted to train me himself, but he mumbled so badly that half the time I didn't understand him. I told myself I would ask the head nurse to review the day's lesson at lunch, but there simply was never any training time.

On my first day, I saw an elderly patient die in the chair from a heart attack (he never should have been given gas in his condition, at his age); another patient having a tooth extracted from the roof of her mouth; and a third patient having all of her upper teeth extracted, a very bloody affair.

Two weeks of that job had me ready to bolt, and I'm sure the dentist shed no tears over my leaving. I still spent my evenings struggling with shorthand, but I now knew of at least two careers that weren't for me. I knew there must be something more suited to my interests and abilities.

CHAPTER TWO

My Golden Gate-way to Opportunity

Living near the San Francisco Bay Area in the mid-1930s, it seemed impossible not to get caught up in the excitement that surrounded the building of the San Francisco-Oakland Bay Bridge and the Golden Gate Bridge, both of which opened in 1937. After they opened, dredging near the Bay Bridge continued for another year to create Treasure Island, the four-hundred-acre site of the San Francisco Golden Gate International Exposition, scheduled to open in February of 1939.

The "San Francisco Fair," as San Franciscans called it, was much more than a fair. To me, it represented a lifting of spirits...something positive, attractive and optimistic after the social unrest and unhappiness of the Depression years. It also served as a turning point for California and the West. So for months, each time we drove across the Bay Bridge, we felt awed by the colorful Land of Oz taking shape below us, filled with palm trees, flowers and beautiful statuary.

One day late in the summer of '38, as I passed over Treasure Island with all its buildings shining in the sun, I experienced an epiphany. "I'll bet that place will need all kinds of workers, even ones who can't take shorthand." Instead of looking through the "help wanted" ads, however, I visited the placement office at U.C. Berkeley. Sure enough, they had plenty of fair openings listed and they sent me to several large companies in San Francisco for interviews.

One of my interviews was with IBM, a company I'd never heard of before, but I felt thrilled when they hired me to demonstrate the company's machines at the IBM pavilion on Treasure Island. They offered me $115 a month, top dollar for the Fair. Plus, to someone who had just flunked out of Merritt School, this job represented a wonderful opportunity to learn all about the business world.

My father worked for the Hawaiian Pineapple Company, which had offices in the Matson Building, one block away from IBM's San Francisco office. When I learned I'd been hired to work at the Fair, I ran down Market Street to tell him the news.

"Daddy, guess what?" I asked, beaming. "Your untrained daughter just got herself a job at the Fair! Now you won't have to support me anymore. How about that?" When I told him my job was with IBM, he was as ecstatic as I was.

"Now, how in the world did you ever land that job? All by yourself, huh?" he asked. "IBM is one of the most prestigious companies in the country." He went on and on about them; he and his company were big customers of theirs and knew all the IBMers I had just met. He extolled IBM's merits, its organization and products.

"You'll get expert training from them." He hugged me. "I'm so proud of you, Ruthie."

When the company told me I would be demonstrating the electric typewriter, I had no idea what I was getting into. I knew I could handle speaking before the public if I practiced, and certainly I had no fear of the typing. For three months, eight of us young women, four from U.C. Berkeley, three from Stanford, and one from the University of Texas, worked in the San Francisco IBM office practicing on our IBM typewriters to increase our speed. To demonstrate the "IBM Electric Writing Machine" at the Fair, we had to type at least 120 words a minute, and most of us typed a mere 50, or so, on a manual typewriter. When we reached 90 words a minute, IBM installed a glass plate directly above the keyboard to increase our finger dexterity and decrease any unnecessary hand movement. This practice served as a prelude to a flashy demonstration we later performed, placing a glass of water on the back of each hand as we typed before an audience.

For some reason, when I reached 90 words a minute, I stayed on that plateau for much too long. I could get no further unless I cheated by typing the same two sentences over and over; "This is a sample of the all electric writing machine. Every mechanical movement is electrically operated." No one knew what I was typing when I finally reached 120 words a minute, and I hoped that no one would find out, either.

Joining the San Francisco IBM office gave me a chance to observe my fellow workers, most of whom I liked very much. It quickly became apparent that the eight of us had been hired in large part for our social graces—our ability to get along with people and deal with just about any situation. Thrown together like that, we could have hated each other, but we got along so well, we spent all our time together—talking about our new job, the people we were meeting in the office, the different techniques of interviewing, and, of course, boys! We struggled together with our typing and even enjoyed competing against each other.

One day, I asked one of my new-found friends, "Where do you think this job will lead us when the Fair closes?"

"I don't know," she replied, "but I'm so happy to have a job that pays this well, I'm going to keep my foot in the door and see what happens."

Another girl added, "Just think, they're allowing us to talk to the public and represent IBM right along with the men. I don't know any other company that does that, and I'm going to try to stay with IBM if they'll have me." None of us had any idea what we wanted to do with our lives at this point, but we planned to enjoy our first learning experience in the real world.

The IBM salesmen were mostly college graduates with business or economics majors from Stanford or U.C. Berkeley. The managers, hard-working but willing to take time to help us neophytes in any way they could, invited us to their sales meetings where we saw how a sales campaign was run and observed the interaction between the sales force and the sales manager.

At one luncheon we attended, it became hard to concentrate when the cigar smoke got as thick as fog rolling in from the Pacific. The meeting inaugurated a big sales campaign by announcing that every IBM salesman who made one hundred per-cent of his sales quota for 1939 would win a trip to Europe. The campaign promotions read, "Will you be onboard or will you be waving goodbye from the pier?"

IBM always believed in slogans, and I was amazed and intrigued by the huge THINK sign and IBM banners hanging on the walls around the room. They excused us right after lunch to return to our class; and I gratefully gulped in the fresh air after escaping the obnoxious cigar smoke.

I found so much to think about in those first weeks of employ-ment, and my co-workers and I often talked amongst ourselves about this company we had joined. The support the company gave us impressed and surprised me.

"Do you realize," I told a new friend, "that as busy as they are, some salesmen are giving us extra training sessions to bring us up to speed on all the IBM machines?"

"Do you think their manager told them to?" one girl asked. We agreed everyone seemed to be happy to help us. Eventually, I posed the question on all our minds: whether or not the company would hire any of us as saleswomen at the end of the Fair, if we were any good at selling the idea of punched cards. We decided we didn't know enough at this point to explore that idea. But, we soon realized that IBM respected each employee, no matter what his or her assignment.

Everyone's helpfulness and concern gave us rookies a sense of security—they really wanted us to succeed. We were part of the team; our job was to demonstrate the machines and create a good impression of IBM before the public. This emphasis on impressing the public proved to be an omen of things to come. Throughout my career at IBM, at every level, especially at the highest, the focus of most of my jobs was very much on public relations.

All Around the Fair

I spent eight and a half months of sheer fun working at the Fair, which opened on February 18, 1939. I not only learned about IBM machines but about other companies' products, as well. More important, I learned how to think on my feet. It was a crash introductory course to the business world, a world I had thought wasn't for me but now found quite fascinating.

I began to rethink my life plans, vague as they were. Maybe I wasn't meant to fall in love and settle down just then. Perhaps I should do something with my life before becoming a bride, if I could ever find the right person!

My parents felt almost more excited than I did about my new job, and they took enormous pride in my progress. They knew I had determination, lots of energy and a competitive spirit I had developed in sports. I just needed to channel it all, and they, as well as IBM, gave me the direction I needed. We all recognized that the IBM training I was getting would take me far beyond where Merritt Business School ever could have taken me.

Visitors could enter the IBM exhibit, a sizable pavilion at the end of the huge hangar-like Hall of Science and Industry building, from all four sides to view all the machines IBM made. At one end of the pavilion stood a platform where we girls demonstrated the electric typewriter. A tall, bulbous thermometer displayed the speed at which we were typing, while an IBM salesman stood beside it giving his sales pitch. This flashy demonstration drew much attention from audiences.

The center part of the exhibit featured all the IBM Accounting Machines, which were then quite large pieces of equipment all actuated by punched cards, the holes of which represented information. Also displayed was the IBM master timeclock, which controlled the many IBM clocks all over Treasure Island.

At the other end of the exhibit stood an "Electric Writing Machine" operating all by itself, attached to the typewriter being demonstrated by one of us to show the versatility of the machine. Also at that end were the Bankproof Machine for sorting checks according to the banks on which they were drawn, and the Test Scoring Machine, widely used in educational circles and military induction centers. All of these IBM machines were of the prewar and pre-computer years line, all developed by IBM's engineers during the period since Mr. Watson had become general manager of the Computing-Tabulating-Recording Company in 1914. In

1924, the company's name was changed to International Business Machines Corporation, better known as IBM.

On the several walls of the IBM exhibit hung an art collection of 79 paintings, each representing a country where IBM did business. These included a style for everyone's taste: primitive, representational, surrealistic, cubist, impressionist, abstract, and others, and the collection proved a great way to pull the public into the exhibit. In fact, this cross section of art attracted so much attention that the demand for information about "IBM's artistic League of Nations" became enormous.

The manager of our exhibit asked for a show of hands of those who had taken any art courses in college. Because I had taken a course in art appreciation my junior year, along with everything else, I suddenly found myself delegated to explaining the art on the walls. I soon learned the true meaning of "a little knowledge is a dangerous thing." My knowledge of art stood about on a par with my shorthand skills.

Explaining the work of Salvador Dali and the other modern painters was beyond me; so what I didn't know, I made up. One day, an unshaven, uncombed middle-aged man dressed in a crinkled Hawaiian shirt followed me around to the last painting listening to my informal and uninformed art lecture. When the crowd dispersed, he lingered to ask me where I had learned my subject.

"Young lady," he said, "do you realize you haven't said one correct thing about these paintings the whole time you've been talking. You don't know a gouache from an oil!" He then reviewed the entire collection with me. I took copious notes as we strolled from painting to painting.

Very grateful, I asked if he were an artist himself or a professor of art. He introduced himself as Boris Aronson, the man who designed the sets for a new play starring Helen Hayes, opening in San Francisco that week. Now that I knew the responsible position he held, I felt more confident about quoting him in my next lecture. The following day he returned to present me with two "house seat" tickets for opening night, which my mother and I enjoyed very much. We learned from the play's program that he was one of Broadway's outstanding set designers.

Next to the IBM exhibit in the Hall of Science, RCA had on display something called a television. Visitors were asked to appear before a television camera to demonstrate this new marvel, but most seemed reluctant or afraid. So, on our breaks, we IBMers would often go "on camera" to help the RCA representative show the public how utterly harmless the equipment was. And what a bunch of hams we were. One day, Bob Hope happened to be in the audience and he got up and did a " Shuffle Off to Buffalo" routine with me.

At the end of our building and directly across from our exhibit, Pacific Gas and Electric had an intriguing diorama built above their exhibit. A huge depiction of early Wild West scenes, it stretched across the entire width of the building. Moving figures played cards, drove a team of horses, planted corn, and participated in other activities. Often, when not showing off on RCA's television during our break, some of us would climb up into the diorama and pretend to kibitz at the poker game, moving our bodies in the same staccato motion as the dummies. A college friend, Jud Callaghan, managed the exhibit and thoroughly enjoyed our antics.

The DuPont exhibit nearby touted an innovation called "nylon stockings," which turned out to be the most important breakthrough of the century for lingerie. Imagine being able to wear a pair of stockings for more than a month or two without getting a run in them! It didn't take manufacturers long, though, to create nylons that ran just as easily as silk stockings.

As the months passed I visited almost all of the exhibits, sometimes lunching on a tuna sandwich at the "Chicken of the Sea" exhibit or on the free handouts from the exhibitors at the Food Hall. Late afternoons after work, we might run over to the south side of Treasure Island to watch the Pan American Clippers take off for Hawaii. We always got a thrill out of that. Night shifts were popular because the dramatic lighting on the sculptures, the fountains, and along the promenades produced a lovely fairyland effect.

Meeting the Watsons

In October, Thomas J. Watson, the IBM president and founder, arrived with Mrs. Watson, their son Tom Jr., daughters Jane and Helen, IBM Vice President F.W. Nichol, and other executives from New York for "IBM Day at the Fair." Before the great day, they all paid a visit to our exhibit. We provincials who had never been to New York City stared in awe at the men's attire: chesterfield coats with velvet collars and homburg hats, which we had seen in movies but never on the streets of San Francisco. We thought the Watson family a strikingly handsome group and very New-Yorkish.

Those of us demonstrators included in the Watson family luncheons that week felt quite privileged. We learned so much from talking informally to the IBM executives, and they in turn seemed to want to know us, too. What little we knew about this family and the company gave us a warm feeling.

After the first luncheon, Mr. Watson turned to me and said, "Miss Leach, you've been telling us about your beautiful fair out here and how much you enjoy your work. Why don't you show my son, Tom, some of your favorite exhibits this afternoon?" Well, how flattering to be asked to escort this tall, dark and handsome man. Plus, I welcomed the opportunity to ask him some questions I'd been pondering.

One was personal. "Tom, why do you carry your hat in your hand all day while the other IBM men wear theirs?"

"I didn't wear a hat to the train in New York, so when we arrived in Chicago, Mr. Nichol took me aside and bought me a homburg, probably at Dad's request, so I'd look like one of the executives—which I'm not!" I sensed the matter had been previously debated, and regretted bringing it up. He really disliked hats unless they were for sailing or for flying in open cockpits. I never saw the homburg again during his visit to San Francisco.

I also learned he'd had something to do with setting up space at the New York World's Fair, a much larger undertaking than our little gem in the Bay. As we walked along that day, he compared the various exhibits with their New York Fair counterparts. "But

I like your amusement center, the Gay Way, better than the New York one." He smiled, "Especially Sally Rand's Nude Ranch."

"You'd better see all that area at night," I said pleasantly, waving my right arm toward the north of the island. "It's much livelier then." I knew he was testing me, and quickly added, "I'm sorry I can't show you the Pan American Clippers which fly from Treasure Island direct to Honolulu once a week, but today's not the day." I thought I'd cut him off rather neatly without seeming a prude.

To celebrate IBM Day, Pierre Monteux conducted the San Francisco Orchestra with Lawrence Tibbett and Grace Moore at the Fair Pavilion. The governor of California and the mayor of San Francisco both spoke, as did Leland Cutler, chairman of the San Francisco Fair, and other dignitaries of the day. We all felt proud to be part of a company that could put on such a fine program. Mr. Watson Sr., of course, ended the day with his talk about IBM.

Mr. Watson, a dignified, gray-haired man, seemed very formal, not only in his dress (he always wore a vest) but in his mannerisms. I guessed he ran the company with a great deal of formality, as well. Even his speech reflected a formal touch, but with character.

On the last evening of the family's visit, I arrived home late. I'd been at a farewell party to send the Watsons on their way by train. I walked in the door at 6:45 to find my mother frantic.

"Tom Watson Jr. has called you twice!" she said, relieved that I'd finally come home. "He wants you to act as his hostess at an impromptu dinner party tonight in San Francisco at the St. Francis Hotel. He said your old friend Walter Wells would pick you up at seven o'clock if you can make it." (Walter lived very near me in Piedmont, across the bay.)

"For heaven's sake," I said as I ran upstairs to change, "I thought I put him on the train with the rest of the Watsons! He doesn't give me much time, does he?"

You'd think by listening to my mother that the Duke of Windsor had invited me to a ball at Buckingham Palace. (My friends were too poor to invite anyone out dinner dancing at the expensive St. Francis.) She helped me break all records to be ready by the time Walter arrived to pick me up. He had been in Tom's sales class in Endicott and told me that Tom had planned to stay behind a day to see what old friends he could find in the area. I didn't know anybody except Walter, but we all had a good time dancing late into the night.

Frankly, I was in awe of Tom since he was the first Easterner I had ever "dated." The more he spoke of his travels to faraway places, the more provincial I felt. His life on the East Coast sounded much more exciting than mine. His informal, relaxed manner was so different from his father's. From the way he talked, I gathered he relished playing Peck's bad boy, as he had with me earlier. I felt flattered to have been invited by him that night, and glad I had passed his test. As the evening ended, I hoped this wouldn't be the last time I saw Tom Jr., and it wasn't.

CHAPTER THREE

Endicott, Here We Come!

Before he left San Francisco that week, Mr. Watson answered the question we'd all been too timid to ask. When he met with all eight of us demonstrators and our Fair manager, Mr. Rumwell, to discuss our future with IBM, he said:

"I want each of you to know how much we have appreciated the fine job you are doing here at the Fair in representing IBM to the public. You are to be congratulated on the amount of IBM information you have assimilated in such a short time and on how well you have displayed your knowledge to the public. Your fellow salesmen assigned here compliment you, and your manager compliments you. So, I know you have made a contribution to our company." Though our hearts were beating fast, there wasn't a sound in the room when he continued.

"I would like to invite you all to join our company on a permanent basis. When the Fair closes, we will send you to Endicott, New York, for further training to become IBM systems service women. You will attend the IBM School there for two or three months to learn the functions and operations of all the machines and how to teach them to IBM customers in the field offices." After extolling IBM's successes, detailing what it had done for the business world, he told us Mr. Rumwell would fill us in later on all the details of our upcoming employment. He finished by saying he hoped we would accept his offer…and then he left the room.

Well, were we ecstatic! With so few business opportunities open to women, that was the most exciting offer in the world to us, and I didn't need to learn shorthand either!

We soon learned that although we would receive no salary during our training, we would get free room and board at the IBM Homestead, the headquarters for VIPs and customers attending the IBM School in Endicott, plus $5.00 a week for expenses. We were all so excited that money didn't seem to matter.

On the first of November we left in style on the City Of San Francisco, a crack streamliner train out of Oakland. What a gala occasion…eight families bidding farewell to their respective "little girls." A supply of our co-workers from the Fair also came to see us off, as did those salesmen who had tried to teach us how to wire the control panels on the big accounting machines so we would shine above our new classmates in Endicott. Adorned with orchids from our IBM Fair manager, we said farewell amid squeals of laughter and excitement until the conductor yelled, "All aboard."

I told my family, "I think I'm more excited about this free trip to New York than about what the future might bring. I'll be like Scarlett O'Hara and 'think about that tomorrow.'" I'd never known any other girl who'd had an opportunity like this.

The eight of us shared two double bedrooms on the train. Memories of life in our college dormitories resurfaced as we joked and laughed together at all hours. After three nights of frolic, we were ready to face the wind and cold of Chicago…or so we thought. But winter took on a new meaning when we climbed off the train in the Windy City early one morning with all of our luggage.

In 1939, when West Coast passengers traveling to points east reached Chicago, they had to change not only trains but stations. The connecting trains usually departed late afternoon from the other station. Since we couldn't avoid this day of lost travel time, we took advantage of it.

"Why don't we invest in taxi fare from one station to the other," someone suggested. "Those taxis look big enough to take our bags, four of us to a cab. Then after we check the baggage, we can spend the day sightseeing."

But we hadn't planned on the freezing weather. We thought we were dressed for winter when we left California in thin coats and open-toed shoes. After checking the bags and walking a block or two, my face felt like ice and my feet were numb. Four of us decided to dash into Marshall Field's huge department store where it was warm and we could breathe again. The other four must have been from hardier stock for they left us saying they would meet us at the train. We planned to continue with our sight-seeing once we thawed out a bit, but our resolution faltered, and instead I called a family friend, Mr. Buell, who invited us to lunch at the elegant Drake Hotel. That still left us two hours to kill, so we had free facials and make-overs in the cosmetics department. We must have been quite a sight in our war paint and drooping orchids when we arrived to meet Mr. Buell. After seeing his expression, the four of us retired to the ladies' room, from which we emerged freshly scrubbed. I think our genial host enjoyed his "painted ladies," and I'm sure we had more fun than the other four girls, who kept warm at the Chicago Art Museum.

The next day, Endicott greeted us with another blast of frigid air. Lucky us...we'd arrived during one of their coldest winter seasons on record. For most of us Westerners, adjusting to minus 10 or 15 degrees wasn't easy. Every day, from the moment we arrived, we wore most of the clothes we'd brought with us, all at the same time. If one of us shouted down the hall: "Today's only a two sweater day," we knew it was going to be mild, like one of California's coldest days.

Our Systems Service Class #448 was composed of the eight of us from the San Francisco Fair, ten young women from the New York Fair, and two from the Canadian IBM Company, Ltd. Our similar backgrounds made us a compatible group; we'd all been hired to demonstrate at the 1939 Fairs. First on our list of assignments was a group picture taken in class by "Fortune" magazine. The photo appeared in a lead article about Mr. Watson and IBM in the January 1940 issue. I'm sure IBM had a hand in placing that picture to show that by 1940 women were already making strides in junior executive positions in large corporations and that T.J. Watson was taking the lead in hiring women for IBM.

Life at the Homestead

During the months at Endicott, we often dined as a group with the class of salesmen who were in session at the same time. The IBM School staff even held dances for us at the Homestead. G.H. Armstrong, head of engineering for IBM, known to all as "Army," loved to call the old dances in his wonderful jovial style. Not only was it fun, it was wholesome fun. As Jeanne Cotten, my roommate from Brooklyn Heights, N.Y., said one night, "Can you believe what fun we had tonight without any liquor, playing all those silly games and dancing old-fashioned dances like the Virginia Reel and the Paul Jones?"

"And," I added, "what I can't get over is how everyone got into the act—faculty and executives, too, and everyone had a great time." Fun though they were, we usually ended these evenings exhausted and hardly fit for the next day's classes.

The Homestead sat on four or five hundred acres in the middle of a nine-hole golf course, a good ten-or fifteen-minute bus ride from Endicott. It was a lovely, home-like place, tastefully furnished, complete with pianos and records of all kinds of music to play on the big Capehart phonograph. Downstairs, there were ping pong, billiards and pool tables, where I spent many a late hour learning the art of shooting pool. Upstairs, three large bedrooms were reserved for executives and VIP visitors. A new wing of about thirty to forty small bedrooms and baths was built for IBM customers and systems service women attending IBM classes. The IBM salesmen were housed at the Hotel Frederick in Endicott. The company's beautiful country club for IBM employees adjoined the Homestead property, providing two golf courses, tennis courts, a swimming pool, bowling alleys, and other facilities for family-oriented activities. In those days, membership cost only $1.00 a year. No wonder those IBM factory workers kept the labor unions out of the Endicott plant. They wouldn't have had a life as elegant as that under union rules.

Endicott in 1940 was a typical old upstate New York town dominated by two large companies: IBM and the Endicott-Johnson Shoe Company. The population was comprised of many

Slavic families attracted there by the shoe company. I found their churches quite fascinating and tried to attend a different one each Sunday.

The IBM factory in Endicott, at that time the company's largest in the U.S., sat right alongside the shoe factory. Directly across the street from our plant stood the IBM School and the handsome red brick engineering building, with its chimes that sounded at intervals.

For three and a half months, we spent every day but Sunday in that school. Every person in the sales force began his career there in a sales class. Every customer engineer learned to maintain the IBM machines in his respective field office by attending engineering classes there. Even the factory workers who wanted to improve themselves were offered the chance to attend classes. Hence, the IBM School became the cultural center of the company in Endicott. At lunchtime and at 5 p.m., music played through amplifiers not only inside the buildings but out over the streets as well. I liked this touch of ending the day on a high note.

Above the front door engraved in letters two feet high was IBM's motto, "THINK." Inside, was a stone staircase designed to put students in an aspiring frame of mind as we climbed to our classrooms. Engraved on the risers were the words, THINK, OBSERVE, DISCUSS, LISTEN, and READ. And indeed, these words became a part of our lives for nearly four months. IBM brought in experts from Harvard and other top schools to teach us everything from new accounting methods to case studies of business practices to time management. IBM teachers, experts on the machines and accounting methods, taught us how to wire the control panels of the machines to direct them as to what kind of information to pick up from the punched cards that actuated the machines.

We studied applications, too, plus undergoing difficult weekly exams. I had never taken accounting in school—I hardly knew a debit from a credit—and I wasn't alone. Eventually, one teacher realized none of us was trained in this field, so he took a week or two and gave us a crash course in accounting, rather than have the whole class fail. We spent four months studying and working hard.

Dear Family—You'll never believe it. Katie and I were the star pupils at wiring plugboards yesterday (due to our late evening training session), and finished our problems so far ahead of the others that the instructor asked us to supervise the others in their wiring. How 'bout that?—Love, Baby

Some brief instruction in public speaking helped us develop our ability to stand before an audience and communicate effectively. We also learned how to teach a class, how to install IBM machines in a customer's office and how to design a punched card and a printed form. All of these functions were part of the job of an IBM systems service woman, a position comparable to today's systems engineer.

In the old days of punched cards, all IBM machines were leased to customers along with the services of a systems service person to perform duties as needed as part of the lease contract. Today, a customer can buy or lease IBM machines but must pay for any systems service work needed.

Aside from learning all the above, I became proficient in singing IBM songs, playing pool and ping pong, and I could bowl over 178. It was great fun, but as my training days drew to an end, I felt ready to move on and test my newly learned skills. Plus, after freezing for three and a half months, I longed for warmer weather.

Christmas Away from Home

The five of us from California knew we wouldn't be getting home for Christmas that year, so we decided to celebrate the holiday in New York City. Since our budgets were so limited, we hadn't planned on any big Christmas dinner. But we didn't care, as long as we saw Fifth Avenue, the Empire State Building and all the tourist spots we'd read about in magazines or had seen in the movies.

The day before Christmas, however, Mr. Watson found out where we were staying (five of us in one room at the New Weston Hotel) and phoned us early in the morning.

"Good morning, girls, this is Mr. Watson speaking."

Out of a sound sleep Betty Lou Yelton asked, "Which Mr. Watson do you think you are?" assuming some idiot had the wrong number, never dreaming that THE Mr. Watson would ever find us in the Big City. Then the tone of her voice changed.

"Oh, oh, yes, Mr. Watson, no, Mr. Watson—I think we can, sir—I will call you right back." He was calling to invite us to his family home for Christmas Eve dinner and to help decorate their tree. What a beautiful way to wake up on Christmas Eve morning.

The Watson family opened their hearts to us just as they had in San Francisco. Gifts awaited each of us at our dinner places, and after dinner Mrs. Watson played the piano while we sang Christmas songs and trimmed their beautiful Christmas tree. What a warm, charming and gracious lady Mrs. Watson was, with such a beautiful twinkle in her blue eyes. She seemed so down-to-earth and confident that you just knew she ruled her family and her household with a firm hand. Her motherly attitude toward each of us endeared her to us.

Mr. Watson monopolized the dinner conversation, which he punctuated with big international names—Hitler, Mussolini, Churchill—and related conversations he had had with each of them. He captivated his audience that night, dazzling us with stories of his personal relationships with all these world leaders.

Autographed portraits of royalty, prime ministers, and other leaders of the day dotted the large walnut-paneled living room. Paintings by several old masters hung on the walls, and the beautiful antique furnishings made the whole room seem like a museum to me. As long as I live, I shall never forget that dinner party in our honor and the kindness the Watsons showed us.

Dear Family—We spent Christmas Eve with the Watsons! Their home is lovely…just as you would imagine…marble, inlaid ceilings, paintings, kings' and queens' pictures all over the place, but in very nice taste and quite 5th Avenueish. Mr. Watson gave each of us perfume and handkerchiefs and we had a lovely dinner with ten million butlers, etc. Tom Jr. and his brother Dickie, dressed in raccoon

coats, took us back to our hotel in the family's Town Car.—
Luff 'n Stuff, Baby

I was pleased and excited to see Tom Jr. again, and he and his younger brother, Arthur (or Dick as everyone seemed to call him), drove us back to the hotel that evening in their big family limousine. They were leaving Christmas morning for Stowe, Vermont, to spend the holidays skiing. Tom let the cat out of the bag when he told us his family was to have left the day before but "something came up at the office..." We knew they had changed their plans on our account and it made the evening even more special.

Before we got out of the car, Tom announced that a table had been reserved for us in the Sert Room of the Waldorf-Astoria as their guests for a Christmas Day dinner. The following evening, we sat in the Watsons' box at the Metropolitan Opera, where we enjoyed "Rigoletto" with Lily Pons as Gilda and Lawrence Tibbett singing the title role. The Watson box was situated in the very center of the "Golden Horseshoe," with J.P. Morgan's box on one side and Mrs. Cornelius Vanderbilt's on the other. Everyone, of course, was dressed to the teeth except the five little maidens from California. You can well imagine how overwhelmed we were with all this generosity and thoughtfulness.

Ready to Take on the World

February 1940, we were deemed ready to get our feet wet. Looking back on the training we received in Endicott, I realized how truly superb it was, from the standpoint that we were prepared for any job that came our way. For three and a half months, our teachers had done their best to mold us into ideal systems service women. At the same time, we had been drinking in the IBM culture.

When the sales manager and Anne van Vechten, head of systems service, arrived in our classroom to hand out assignments, I prayed silently, "Oh please, please give me one of the jobs in California, at least somewhere not too far from my family and friends."

But we Californians didn't fare as well as the Eastern and Canadian members of our class, who were all assigned offices near their homes. Only two of us were to return to San Francisco and Oakland, while the rest were scattered all over the country.

After having formed close bonds of friendship, first at the Fair and later in Endicott, the time had come for tears and farewells. The next day, I was to leave for my new assignment in Atlanta, Georgia.

Before we spread out to our various destinations, six of the remaining Californians met in New York at the Rainbow Room in Rockefeller Center for one last cocktail together.

"Let's click glasses to our future, whatever it brings," I said, "and promise to stay in touch with each other." And we did.

One of the salesmen from a class in Endicott traveled down to New York to take me to dinner and dancing that evening at the Pennsylvania Hotel where Glenn Miller was playing. Then that cheerful soul bounced me over to the Stork Club (my first visit there) to raise my spirits before putting me on the sleeper for Washington, DC, where I was to meet the two lucky girls who'd drawn assignments in California for a one-day visit to our nation's capital.

All night on the sleeper I mentally wrote a telegram to my parents. "NOT COMING HOME STOP ASSIGNED TO ATLANTA STOP MISERABLE"...No..."WISH I WERE HOME"...No... "SHOULD BE INTERESTING STOP LOVE RUTHIE"

I sent it when I arrived in Atlanta.

Our visit to Washington was a whirlwind sightseeing tour, "On the Town" with three girls instead of three sailors. We conned a cab driver into showing us the sights for $10 (divided by three). He was extremely knowledgeable about his city, which he really enjoyed showing off. Our feet ached from climbing up and down so many stairs—to the top of the Washington Monument, the Lincoln Memorial, the Capitol, the White House, the churches, parks, and monuments galore. But we loved every minute of it.

Washington was, and still is, one of the most beautiful cities in the world. After that tour, I wished I had been assigned there instead of where I was going. I really knew nothing about Atlanta except it was in the South. Well, I'd wanted a warmer climate, and Atlanta was certainly that, especially in those days before air conditioning. After more tearful farewells at Union Station, I was really on my own.

CHAPTER FOUR

Unchaperoned in Atlanta

Alone in the dining car of the train to Atlanta, I began to feel like an explorer. I always felt happiest when embarking on a new adventure, whether it was mastering a new sport, driving a truck over dried-up river beds, researching the Mayan civilization, or learning how to wire a control panel for an IBM accounting machine.

Gazing out the windows of that train, however, I suddenly realized just how far I would be from home and friends. Would I like living in the South? What kinds of new friends would I make? And what about my new job, would I perform well? As I wrestled with these doubts, a couple sat down opposite me. We introduced ourselves and began making small talk.

"Have you been to Atlanta before?" I asked.

They wasted no time filling me in on their view of this southern city. "When the train stops in Atlanta, don't bother getting off. There's absolutely nothing to see in that place. It's a miserable town, so dirty, with coal dust everywhere. Even the politics are dirty. Segregation is a messy affair all over the South..." And they went on and on, pointing out every little negative thing they could think of. I began to feel sorry I'd asked the question in the first place. That dreary travelogue was my first introduction to my future home.

My own impression upon arrival could not have been more different. The city had been spruced up for the gala world premiere at the local Fox theater of the long-awaited movie of Margaret Mitchell's book, *Gone with the Wind*, with its award-winning cast of Clark Gable, Vivian Leigh, Leslie Howard, and Olivia DeHavilland. The movie is still considered by many to be one of the best ever made.

The day I arrived in Atlanta, most of the natives were still in period costumes for the occasion. Shop windows sported true "Gone With The Wind" fashions, making me feel like I'd stepped back in time. "What a glamorous place to work," I thought. "And how kindly the people treat a total stranger." I soon realized, however, that the veneer of politeness didn't extend to genuine warmth. It quickly became apparent that as a single lady living alone and lacking the proper social credentials, I was to be shut out of "polite society."

On my own away from my family for the first time, and earning only $100 a month, I soon learned what a budget meant. (Once I got to know my manager better, I spoke to him about the matter of earning $15 a month less than I had earned the year before. Was that any way for big business to operate?)

Mr. Clemmons, the IBM Atlanta manager, was a stern boss with little if any sense of humor who seemed wedded to his job. When I walked into his office to report for work the first day, he seemed surprised.

"But I haven't received anything from headquarters about you. Besides, I already have a systems service woman, and one is about all we can handle down here."

I never felt so unwanted in my life. If I'd had any money with me, I would have taken the next train west. It wasn't my place to tell him what he didn't know yet: that his lovely red-haired systems service woman, Eliza Rose, was leaving to be married. He should have received a letter from Anne van Vechten, the head of systems service, explaining the whole situation. Apparently, the letter had been delayed. It arrived in the next mail, and I belatedly joined the IBM Atlanta Sales Department.

At first, Mr. Clemmons had no idea what to do with me, since Eliza was still on the job. So I busied myself learning about life in that office: what an IBM service bureau does, what an office manager manages, how a telephone switchboard works, and other minor but important details. Then I decided that all the cabinets needed a good cleaning out. Atlanta was a city of coal-burning furnaces that created a sooty smog over the town, and dust settled everywhere. They hadn't hired me for this kind of work, but the office needed a good dusting and someone had to do it.

Early in my stay I learned to drink Coca Cola, the beverage of choice in the South. Though I disliked it, everyone seemed to drink it at every hour of every day, almost like a social ritual. When I visited the offices of IBM customers, they would greet me with, "Won't you have a Coke?"

Then I had to learn how to speak "Southe'n." When I first started teaching an IBM class, my students would ask the same questions over and over just to hear me talk. There was much giggling and little learning, I'm afraid. In desperation, I enlisted the help of the IBM switchboard operator, Eulalia, who patiently taught me how to drop the "g's" on word endings, to accent the first syllables of such words as "INsurance" and "JUly", and to greet friends with "Hey, honey, how'yewww?" Soon I picked up a real "Southe'n" accent and used it unconsciously in my work.

Dear Family—It seems the only way I can talk with the locals here so that they can understand me is to speak their language. The phrases I've picked up would amuse you. I can just see myself greeting friends on the street in San Francisco with a big "Hey!" instead of the usual "how have you been?" Instead of "a week from next Monday," we Southerners merely say "Monday week." Shall I bring an interpreter home with me?—Baby

All Work and No Play

I learned quickly that at IBM, a forty-hour workweek meant nothing if your job was not finished. Many a weekend I worked with my salesman and customers on difficult jobs. New Year's Eve 1940 and the first weekend of 1941 I spent helping get the payroll out at the large Davison-Paxon department store when their employees went on strike.

Working at night in a store with counters shrouded in sheets was spooky; it reminded me of a mystery story I once read. Then to make matters worse, I didn't know that the door to the IBM machine records room where I was working was self-locking. It took a number of two a.m. phone calls to get me out.

Another time, one of our bank customers had trouble getting a special accounting job to work properly, so we worked day and night, through the weekend to solve the problems. Working late didn't bother me then, as I didn't know anyone outside the office to pal around with anyway.

The biggest IBM account I worked on in Atlanta was the National Public Health Records of the U.S. Department of Health. In 1941, people were asking for copies of their birth certificates so they could apply for defense plant work, only to discover that they had been declared "stillborn" (dead, at birth). I was assigned to help get to the root of this problem. After some research, we found that many midwives had made the same mistake over and over again, thinking "stillborn" meant the same thing as "born."

Statistical analysis was a perfect application for IBM machines. I directed an early statistical study at the National Public Health Records of the spread of syphilis and gonorrhea for the entire United States, the results of which appeared in print all over the nation. Never before had anyone been able to set up interstate systems to gather such information so quickly in order to maintain a check on the spread of disease. It was the IBM system that did it, and I was very proud of that job.

One day in the middle of that assignment I received a phone call at the Public Health machine records department.

"What are you doing, Ruth?" the voice on the line asked.

Thinking it was the salesman assigned to this account, who called every day about its status, I answered proudly, "Well, I've just finished the syphilis report, and I'm about to start the gonorrhea study."

"WWHHATT??" It was Tom Watson Jr., calling me from Anniston, Alabama, from the Air Force base. "I'm coming to Atlanta tomorrow, so I checked to see if I knew anyone in the Atlanta office. I was surprised you were there, but I'm even more surprised by your project."

I was flustered, but tried to recover. "Well, I'm surprised to learn that you're a flier. When did you enlist?" He wanted to know if I would have dinner with him and an Air Force friend the next day, and would I ask another girl to join us.

"Tom," I said, "I haven't been here long enough to know any girls to ask, but I'll try to find one." I never did, so I dined with two handsome lads in uniform and took turns dancing with each of them.

My systems service assignments constantly challenged me, each one different from the last. I loved my work, even when I was the only woman on the job, as I was when I worked with the trust officers of the First National Bank. At most companies, the man in charge of machine records was the financial officer, so that's who I'd work with. Working with men never bothered me because I felt I knew my job, but I found I often had to prove it to those men who were obviously reluctant to work with me.

My job required not only skill but also a great deal of patience and tact. The art of getting along with people seemed to me the most important thing one could learn in business. And having a sense of humor helped, too.

In 1941, particularly in the South, there were very few women working on assignments like mine. I understood, however, that some people had trouble accepting the unfamiliar.

The Atlanta IBM office set-up consisted of three women in the front office: Mrs. Barnett, the office manager; Eulalia at the switchboard; and myself, plus Mr. Clemmons, the sales manager. The five or six salesmen spent most of their time in their sales territories. So I seemed to always get to handle the extra-curricular jobs that came up from time to time. Sometimes those proved to be interesting and exciting.

The University of Georgia in Athens, Georgia, for example, set up a traveling art exhibit sponsored by IBM, and I was assigned to assist their art department. I planned to remain at the campus through the opening night to represent the company. The IBM salesman who handled the university's account also planned to be there. To my surprise, the exhibit included some of the same paintings I had lectured about at the Fair in San Francisco. I helped the university plan a reception for preview night, publicize the event and decide which VIPs to invite. It felt like old times, talking about "my San Francisco paintings" and representing IBM in the art world.

During my stint in Atlanta, Mr. Clemmons became ill and had to take a month's leave, so a few of us took over some of his duties. The office manager handled much of the paperwork, while I took his phone calls. Sometimes, I would help Eulalia at the switchboard, often solving wiring problems over the telephone or satisfying an irate customer about some service problem. With the salesmen out most of the day selling, the three of us–Eulalia; Mrs. Barnett; and I–were left to run the office...great experience for me.

When Mr. Clemmons returned and reviewed all our weekly reports made during his absence, he called me in to pay me my first real compliment.

"Ruth," he said, "I've trained many men and systems service people, but I've never seen one who stood up so well under what you've gone through since you arrived in Atlanta." (I should have asked him right then about a raise.)

A Different Culture

While I enjoyed the variety of work I was doing, I felt uncomfortable living in a community with segregation laws. Growing up in California had not prepared me for the strong feelings about race that I found in Atlanta. I could sympathize with the social outsider, as I felt very much like an outsider myself.

Social strata in the South were based on local background and tradition. My social standing in California carried no weight in Atlanta, so meeting people was difficult. When Eliza left to get married, I moved into her room at the Georgian Terrace Hotel. One day, a nice elderly couple, Judge and Mrs. Rosser, who lived on my same floor finally spoke to me, "Are you visiting here, Miss Leach?"

"No," I replied, "I'm living here now, working for IBM in their office down on Peachtree Street."

They were taken aback by that information. Mrs. Rosser confessed, "Frankly, I am astonished that your family are not here to chaperone you. How could they have sanctioned your making such a trip from California alone?"

With someone as enmeshed in the social customs of the South as Mrs. Rosser, I found it difficult to discuss the subject any further. In my mind, she belonged to another era.

While the general citizens of Atlanta seemed an honest group, I couldn't say the same for the political leaders. Graft and corruption were, unfortunately, fairly common in those days.

Dear Family—Well, everyone here is talking about our ex-governor...the Crook. On his last night in office, he pardoned 80 convicts, 22 of whom were murderers serving life terms. Can you imagine such an awful thing? Some of them were horrible cases, too. Then it came out that since December he has pardoned a good 300! He knew he was washed up politically I guess, so he wanted to clean up enough cash to retire.—Love, Baby

The Georgian Terrace was the only affordable place to live that I could find near the office. When I took over Eliza's room, I also inherited her roommate, Bertha Nix, a secretary to the architectural department of Georgia Tech and at least ten years older than I. Bertha possessed the most delightful sense of humor I have ever known, and because of that we got along very well. In spite of that, I still had no one to socialize with, as she always went home to Albany, Georgia on the weekends to tend to her ailing mother.

Living in a small hotel room, with one small closet each and a bathroom way at the end of the hall, was not my idea of home, even a home away from home. But Bertha and I made the most of it. On sweltering hot sticky nights we had no ventilation, and armies of cockroaches performed maneuvers under our beds.

Bertha introduced me to a neighborhood diner where I could get wholesome dinners for 50 cents. Lunches were just 35 cents at the S & W Cafeteria near the office, which left me 15 cents for a Toddle House breakfast of juice, toast, and coffee. Room rent was

$60, and food costs were about $30 a month. The remaining $10 of my pay check had to cover my clothes, cleaning, transportation (I walked everywhere), movies and taxes! But I was too proud to write home for money; I wanted to prove to my family that I could earn my own living. So I learned how to be a survivor.

It wasn't a great life then in Atlanta, but I kept telling myself, "This is good discipline for me, and I should be a better person for it someday."

Socially, it was a disaster, such a lonely life during those first nine months. I went to movies alone, walked the neighborhood a lot, and even watched nationally ranked "Bitsy" Grant and others through a chain link fence play my beloved game of tennis when I didn't have the price of admission. How I wished I could have found a fellow tennis player with two racquets, as I certainly couldn't afford to buy one.

I made a mental note to tell the IBM bosses in New York, when I knew them better, never to send a young woman too far away from her family and friends, especially to cities whose customs and traditions make it so difficult to meet people. Single men, I thought, found a readier acceptance. Mr. and Mrs. Clemmons graciously invited me to their home on occasion, but I wanted a life outside of IBM, and I was determined to make one, too.

My years as a Camp Fire Girl and a counselor at the Piedmont Girls Camp in the Sierras had taught me to appreciate the beauties of the wilderness and of outdoor life and had instilled in me a lifelong love of nature. When I read about the Appalachian Trail Club in the local paper, I joined up for something to do on weekends.

Trail Club meetings took me out of my hotel room and into the countryside for some spectacular hikes. The members I met were always stimulating—professional people, medical doctors, professors, botanists, lawyers, and more. No matter whom I walked with, I always learned something new. Most of them, like myself, came from other parts of the country.

The members were used to talking while they hiked, and though by nature I'm a talkative person, on my first hikes I had little to say. I would stop often to admire the beauty of nature as an excuse to rest my unconditioned body. It was all I could do to pant up the hilly trails in silence; I became an excellent listener.

Despite my encounters with mosquitoes, fleas, lightning bugs, and chiggers on some of the overnight trips, I enjoyed every outing. But I always came back so stiff and sore that I welcomed any inactive Sundays as a chance to recuperate before starting another work week.

Still, I was lonely and unhappy. I did a lot of soul searching, wondering just where this life in Atlanta would take me. IBM had put a lot of time, effort, and expense into training me, and I thought the least I could do was to give Atlanta a try for a year before asking for a transfer back to the West Coast. At Christmas 1940, I finally got a $25 a month raise, which helped some.

By the end of that year a friend from California introduced me by mail to a gentleman from a prominent Atlanta family of long standing and impeccable credentials. Mike May had just returned to his native city after an absence of ten years, during which time all the girls he once knew had married, so he was delighted to have a blue-eyed blonde from California to escort to his favorite haunts.

When he introduced me properly to his friends, I was suddenly socially acceptable. Despite their previous reservations, even Judge and Mrs. Rosser extended very warm hands of friendship. It was like meeting them for the first time, even though we had been speaking to each other for about a year. That was Atlanta in 1941.

Being a "people" person and very competitive in sports, I really needed a social life, and at last I had one. My new friend Mike often took me to dinner at the Piedmont Driving Club (Atlanta was a "club" town then), to the famous "Nine O'Clocks," a traditional Atlanta black-tie affair, and to other social gatherings. The one I liked best was the Friday night group, which gathered at Fritz Orr's lovely home to play badminton, poker dice, backgammon, and other games. It was there I met some of the trust officers of the First National Bank where I was working to help install IBM equipment.

Looking for a Change

I was beginning to enjoy life in Atlanta, but I still yearned to return home. So I wrote a letter to Anne van Vechten, head of systems service, requesting a transfer to the West Coast.

In the spring of 1941, Mr. Clemmons announced that Mr. and Mrs. Watson were to pay the Atlanta office a visit. I helped set up the luncheon in their honor; everyone in the office attended and brought their wives, too. It was the Watsons' custom to visit as many offices as time would permit, to meet as many IBMers as they could. Most IBM employees were in such awe of this man that they were afraid to speak, so luncheons like these could be pretty dull unless a ham like me was around. I had the advantage of having met the Watsons on several occasions, so I felt relaxed in their presence.

"Tell us about your visits to other offices in the South, Mr. Watson," I asked just to get the ball rolling. He went on for awhile, then looked down the table at me.

"Miss Leach (he never called me by any other name), the new accent you've acquired since I last saw you in Endicott must mean you have been teaching a lot of customers here," he said. "Now what do you teach first, machine operation or applications?"

I wondered why he asked that particular question. Did he plan to rewrite the teaching manuals? How should I answer him?

"Mr. Watson," I replied, "customers come to our office to learn how to operate the machines. So I teach my students the function and operation of those machines. Then, if time permits, I teach them the applications. Or the person in charge of the machine records department at their company can teach them applications after they've learned to operate the equipment."

That got his adrenaline going, and he retorted, "But don't you think applications is the more important subject to teach than machines?"

"No, I think machines are more important to teach at this point in their IBM education."

Well, did anyone ever disagree with Mr. Watson? Mr. Clemmons, I knew, was having a fit over this discussion, and others squirmed in their seats. Perhaps I spoke too much, but that was the way I felt. If he objected to my opposing him, maybe he'd just fire me on the spot, and I could go back home where I belonged. Instead, he proceeded to lecture us on how important it was to teach applications, then he went on to discuss other things about IBM and the world situation. The whole afternoon turned out quite pleasant.

One afternoon in April, shortly after the Watsons' visit, Eulalia stopped me as I returned from a customer's office. She was very excited.

"Ruth, you're to call Mr. Watson in New York the moment you get in." Of course this was a joke; I wasn't about to return that call. Why would he be phoning me? So Eulalia dialed him herself, then handed the telephone to me.

It was Mr. Watson, all right, saying, "Miss Leach, I called to ask if you will come to Endicott this summer to help teach a sales class of IBM accountants from various offices." I was stunned, first to think he would call me personally, and second, to think I would be qualified to teach a class of accountants!

"But Mr. Watson," I said, "I've already written to Miss van Vechten for a transfer to the West Coast."

"Now, I will give you every opportunity to visit your family there if you will come to Endicott this summer." (Once a salesman, always a salesman.)

Well, I thought, it will be for just the summer. Besides, my mother was coming east for a visit, and we could travel to Endicott together so she could see where I started my IBM training. Of course I accepted the challenge, but I added, "Now don't forget your promise." And he never did, either.

When I told my friend Mike about Mr. Watson's phone call, he hurried over to my hotel and asked me to marry him. I hadn't expected this, and though I liked him enormously as a good friend, I wasn't interested in marrying him...or anyone else for that matter, at this point.

Atlanta had been an enlightening experience for me—a different society, almost like another country. But I never would have been happy living there. The values and mores were too different from mine. Besides, the high humidity and terribly hot summers, to say nothing of the coal dust in winter, never agreed with me. So I said farewell to a very dear set of friends, all of whom I had met through soft-spoken Mike. I felt particularly sad saying goodbye to him. When I left for Endicott, of all places, I truly believed the assignment was just for the summer. How wrong I was.

CHAPTER FIVE

Endicott Again

This time around, my life at the Homestead proved quite different from my first visit. For one thing, I came as the teacher, not the student. For another, rather than having me live at the Homestead with my students, Mr. Watson arranged for me to share a little white cottage nearby with Mary Bunce, one of the original systems service women hired from Smith College in 1935. Like me, Mary had been invited to Endicott to teach the sales classes. Imagine our delight when we learned that not only were we to have quiet and privacy away from the crowd, but also Mr. Watson planned to let us fix up the cottage in any fashion we wanted.

We decorated freely, replacing carpets and flooring, blinds and bedding. We even purchased new appliances. It took forever to accomplish this in the little enclave of Endicott, but the results were worth it. We had a place we loved to come home to, a place where we could escape the chatter of the Homestead, since we had to study hard nearly every night just to stay ahead of our students.

Mr. Watson, ever solicitous, suggested we get a dog for protection. So, we got a puppy and named him "Bunlea," a combination of our last names. Sadly, we never had a chance to train him properly. He developed a problem with seizures, so after numerous visits to the veterinarian and many bottles of pills, we realized he was getting worse and must be put down. Poor Bunlea didn't live long enough to provide us any protection, but fortunately, we didn't need any.

Mary, from Hartford, Connecticut, possessed a booming voice and a somewhat overpowering, aggressive personality. Most of her assignments in IBM had been teaching in the New York area. Though we had different personalities, I enjoyed her willingness to adventure out on weekends whenever we could slip away in her car. We visited her parents in Hartford, explored New England as much as we could, and even drove to Montreal with my mother during her visit to Endicott.

Most weeknights, we stayed up until two or three in the morning, studying applications and preparing for the next day's lessons. I tried to stay at least one page ahead of that brilliant class of "Phi Beta Kappas," hoping my lack of accounting knowledge didn't show.

During the spring and long hot summer, free time was rare. When I could steal some, I tried to play tennis. On her visits to Endicott, our boss, Anne van Vechten, managed to play some sets with me. We both loved the game, and soon became good friends over the net. I enjoyed her keen sense of humor and stories about the early days of systems service and how she became the first head of that department.

Anne had attended Bryn Mawr College, then gone on to a secretarial school in New York City. While there, she had an assignment to interview the CEOs of three large companies. She wrote and asked Mr. Watson for an interview, having known his daughter Jane at school. Anne explained her assignment to him and asked what qualifications a person would need to succeed in the business world.

During the interview she remarked, "You know, Mr. Watson, young women need opportunities in the business world, other than secretarial, and I think IBM and other big companies should make some jobs available to women."

The remark stuck in Mr. Watson's mind during the whole interview. As they finished their chat, he said, "Miss van Vechten, you're hired." That surprised her completely, considering she'd come in to interview him, not to ask for a job.

"But what would I do?" she asked.

"During our brief discussion, you have prompted me to

consider using women in roles other than secretarial," he told her, "and I think women would make good 'systems' people, helping to install the IBM method of accounting in customer's offices. We could start a training school in Endicott, then hire twenty-four other girls, train them, then place them in our field offices as systems service women. And you can help me."

A few days later, he made it official. Thus, Systems Service for Women was born in the spring of 1935, and Anne was among the first group to be trained in this capacity. Up until then, salesmen or the service bureau managers had handled the systems service jobs.

Twenty-four college graduates joined Anne, from Cornell, Wellesley, Vassar, Mt. Holyoke, Bryn Mawr, Smith, and other colleges in the East. They reported to Endicott in July of 1935. Another systems service class convened in 1936 and another in 1937. Then came the "Fair" girls of 1939—my class, and still another, larger group in 1940. As the years passed, the training became more professional.

Starting up the Corporate Ladder

September, 1941

Dear Family—Last Tuesday, Charlie Love (Secretary of Education, head of IBM school in Endicott), told me to take the sleeper down to New York City, as I was wanted at Headquarters the next day. I was fighting a cold and spent a sleepless night on the train wondering what or where I was going next...or why I was being called to the corporate offices to be chastised.

When I arrived, I went right to Annie Van's office and she forewarned me that Mr. Watson planned to offer me her job, as she was leaving to be married. I almost swooned right there. By the time I got to T.J.'s office a little before noon, I was all mixed up inside about what to do. I thought about all the glamour of living in New York City, the contacts I had made, and the experience and opportunity this presented. Then I thought about the work itself and the responsibility and politics involved.

I also pondered whether or not I could handle this big job and decided that he's taking the chance—he and the rest of his executives chose me for the job, so they're more or less responsible. Of course, I shall do the best I can and all that...so, I decided that the work won't bother me at all, and Annie will be there for some time yet to help me.— Love, Baby

That restless night on the Delaware Lackawanna sleeper was the first of many sleepless nights on that train, which over the next three years became my second home. I began calling it the Lackawanna-Lackasleepa.

I felt happy to learn I'd done nothing wrong: Rather, Anne had done something right. The secret had escaped that Anne planned to marry Douglass Coupe, a delightful young Army lieutenant whom I had met. During their courtship, I had helped Anne write to him during one of her stays in Endicott. We even put a fish hook inside one letter (to help her hook him)!

I'd known they were contemplating an announcement soon, but I had no idea she wanted to be relieved of her duties so that she could remain in New York City to be near Doug.

With only Anne and myself in his office, discussing Anne's contribution to IBM history, Mr. Watson turned to me and said, "Miss Leach, we have been reviewing the names of various systems service women and have come to the conclusion that you should be selected to replace Miss van Vechten as Secretary of Education for Women. Would you accept?" I was flabbergasted.

"But do you really think I'm qualified, Mr. Watson? I haven't been in the company very long—only two and a half years."

He replied, "I've seen you in operation at the San Francisco Fair, in Atlanta, and in Endicott. I know you are qualified, and so do your bosses from the Fair, Mr. Clemmons in Atlanta, and Mr. Love in Endicott."

I had to sort out quickly what I wanted to do. Why should I want to go home to California, where I would be doing the same work I did in Atlanta, when life was so exciting here in New York? Here I could make a real contribution, maybe become an executive, as Anne seemed to be. It didn't take me long to say yes.

My acceptance didn't surprise Mr. Watson. "I would like you to start by visiting all the IBM offices in this country where we have systems service women, to evaluate their work. Interview their managers to find out how they evaluate the systems service women. Don't be afraid to make constructive suggestions. Also, whenever you are out on the Pacific Coast, I want you to feel free to visit your family and friends for a day or two. You see, I remember my promise.

"Now, let's keep this under our hats until graduation, at which time I would like to make the announcement. Don't even discuss this with Miss Bunce or anyone else." Mr. Watson always liked to surprise IBMers with announcements like this, and a graduation with several hundred people present was just the kind of audience he liked.

It delighted me not to say anything to Mary Bunce about my exciting news, knowing her volatile nature: I preferred to let someone else tell her about my promotion. I knew she'd feel cheated since she'd been in the company longer than I.

Dear Family—Everyone is going to be so surprised at my promotion they'll drop dead! Most of all will be Mary, and I shall dread being around her when it all happens. She keeps saying "after school's over we'll do" this and that, and "I've engaged a laundress to come to the cottage after school closes," etc. Then I'd find myself saying "don't you like these shoes? They'll be so good for walking to the office." When I realize what I've said, I fumble around trying to squeeze out of it! You know me...never could keep a secret.—Luff, Baby

Two nights in a row on the sleeper going and coming from that eventful meeting was too much for my ailing body. My symptoms turned into a full-blown cold and a cough. Mr. Watson called the head of the IBM school and told him to take me to the Sayre Clinic in Pennsylvania for a complete check- up. The dark circles under my eyes that day in New York must have been vivid, and I know I coughed too much, so I'm sure he had second thoughts about my health.

I'd never been in a hospital before, so I reveled in the attention of a whole herd of handsome interns. They asked me about my medical history, but I had none as I had always been healthy. In the end, they decided I was simply exhausted: too many late nights studying.

After two days and nights of sleep, I felt raring to go, but I had to remain for a week for continued rest. Finally, two interns drove me back to the Homestead, all revived and ready for anything.

In October 1941, at the graduation dinner in Endicott, Mr. Watson ended the festivities by saying, "Now ladies and gentlemen, I have an announcement to make. After being in charge of systems service and education for women these past six years, Miss van Vechten has made a big decision in her life. She is leaving IBM soon to be married to a young Army lieutenant, Douglass Coupe. Her accomplishments are many, and we thank her for all the many contributions she has made to this company. We wish her much happiness in her future life." The popular Anne received a standing ovation.

Then he paused dramatically and said, "After much consideration, we have decided that Miss Ruth Leach, your instructor here in Endicott, will replace Miss van Vechten in New York City at the end of her duties here."

As I had anticipated, this announcement was met with complete surprise. Most surprised was Mary Bunce, who left the company shortly afterwards. But I could only think, "Do I have enough experience to handle the job?" Perhaps my willingness to disagree with Mr. Watson at the luncheon in Atlanta had something to do with my selection.

I soon learned that working at World Headquarters meant facing one huge challenge after another. The first, and one of the most stressful I ever encountered, was making my first acceptance speech before the crowd of five hundred that night.

With dry mouth and shaking hands, I stood up and spoke. "Ladies and gentlemen, thank you so very much for your response and good wishes in my new assignment. It is, indeed, a terrific challenge, and I can't wait to meet it head on. My biggest problem here is that I have a very tough act to follow..." And so began my speechmaking days in IBM.

If I'd known my new job entailed so much public speaking, I might have thought twice about accepting it. Each speech proved more challenging than the one before. With all the courses I'd taken in college, why hadn't I taken a course in public speaking, drama, or debating?

CHAPTER SIX

New York, New York!

Though I'd failed to make it back to San Francisco, I had managed to escape the confinement of tiny Endicott. Plus, I was moving to a place many people considered the most exciting city in the world—New York. And what an incredibly glamorous and exciting place to be in the 1940s. Fabulous museums, art galleries, the opera, music galore, top fashions, theater, and other cultural programs, colleges and universities...all gathered together in one city. And, unbelievable as it seems today, the city was safe and clean. I walked everywhere, day and night, even through Central Park. I became so wrapped up in my new hometown, I entirely forgot my yearning for the West Coast.

Old friends from college days already lived in New York, and once we entered the war, several young men I'd known in school, now in uniform, came through en route to Europe. I must have had USO night at my apartment nearly twice a month.

Miraculously, with the help of an old family friend, I found myself ensconced in one of the most elegant apartments I had ever seen. Beautifully furnished, in exclusive Sutton Place at the end of East 56th Street, it had a wood-burning fireplace, and mirrored walls that reflected Manhattan's skyline and part of the East River. What's more, I could walk the six blocks across town to my new office in IBM's World Headquarters at 57th and Madison Avenue. I called this arrangement heaven!

The apartment had briefly been the home of a newly married couple who suddenly realized they'd made a big mistake and left town to go their separate ways. That explained the new mono-grammed towels and linens, and all the unused equipment in the kitchen.

An old college friend from California, Jane Parrish, also with IBM, also needed a place to live. She, too, had been promoted to World Headquarters, as a special representative for hospital accounting. So we shared the apartment and the $150 a month rent, cheap even then considering the location and dramatic decor.

Life in New York City proved exciting, but oh so expensive.

Dear Family—What a town this is! Money, money, money! In five days, I plunked down about $200 for rent, hotels, taxis, etc....and it seems every time I turn around, someone has a big mitt outstretched. Janey and I are now on "economy measure #234"—saving electricity. In fact, we practically run around in the dark.—Baby

Jane and I felt quite daring on our own in Manhattan, although two doormen guarded us securely, one at the front and one at the side entrance to our building. And what a joy to have our own well-equipped kitchen, so we could cook meals at home and save money on eating out. We even had a cozy living room in which to entertain, complete with a small piano, which we both enjoyed playing. We loved our life and our adventures in the Big Apple. Particularly, we loved our "snazzy" digs, and so did our friends.

Two blocks away lived another close college friend, Augusta Dabney, married then to Kevin McCarthy—both of them aspiring actors. They had met at the American Academy of Dramatic Art in New York City, then landed their first big roles with Raymond Massey in "Abe Lincoln In Illinois," which toured all over the U.S. Augusta and I saw each other frequently when I was in town, and I enjoyed meeting her and Kevin's friends, also struggling actors, among them, Montgomery Clift, Mona and Karl Malden, Roddy McDowell, Edmond O'Brien, and composer/lyricist Alec Wilder from our class at Berkeley.

I knew nothing about the acting profession, but seeing them as much as I did, I could sympathize with the hard struggle these dedicated artists went through before getting their first big break. I cooked spaghetti dinners for Augusta and Kevin and their friends, listening to their "shop" talk—reviewing current plays and musicals, who was casting for new shows, who had snagged what juicy part. These little soirées brought a new dimension to my life in the big city and a better understanding of what a career in the theater entails. And as my company called on me increasingly to represent them before the public, I began to appreciate the applicability of the actor's art to the business environment. With each speech I gave, I gained greater respect for the profession my actor friends had chosen.

All that aside, the most exciting part of living in New York City was working at the IBM World Headquarters, spending each day at the center of all the action, where company executives made significant decisions...sometimes before my very eyes.

I'd never had a secretary before, nor had I ever written important letters to important people. Thank heavens the company appointed Lillian Schumm to my office from the secretarial pool. The first morning she greeted me with, "Good morning, Miss Leach. What would you like me to do for you today?"

"Oh, I'm not sure," I told her. "You see—I've never had a secretary before—and I've never given dictation. So, I guess you and I will have to start from scratch!" We had a good laugh, and that eased our nervousness. I asked what kind of files Miss van Vechten kept and what type of correspondence she conducted. Anne had been too busy getting married to show me what she did in this busy job I now had.

Miss Schumm, highly experienced (and a whiz at shorthand!) knew exactly what to say and how to write letters tactfully. She taught me a great deal, and I welcomed her kind assistance and intuitiveness during those early days.

Another Holiday with the Watsons

That first winter of 1941-42 in New York, the Watsons invited Jane Parrish and me to Thanksgiving dinner at their home. Of the seventeen people gathered around the large table, only three were men, Mr. Watson, and his two sons. The rest were female relatives, and a few strays like us thrown in.

When the butler announced dinner, Mr. Watson took my arm and said, "Shall we go in to dinner now?"

To my surprise, I found myself seated on his right. I became panicky when they served the first course: a persimmon! I had no idea how to eat it. Trying to appear nonchalant, I toyed with the oddly shaped utensils before me while stealing glances around the table to see what others were doing. Then my host graciously said, "You know, I never can tell whether or not I am eating these things correctly."

"Now I have the same trouble," I said, relieved. "I'll let you try first, and I'll follow what you do." I knew he had said that to ease my predicament, and I soon wished I'd followed his lead more carefully. Rather than spooning out just the inside, I ate the skin and all, until my mouth puckered so I wondered if I would ever talk again.

After dinner, who should our hosts ask to entertain but Jane and me, so we gamely performed our duets on the piano, singing along with ourselves.

At the end of the day, the Watsons proudly showed us the 1920 electric car they'd bought from Jimmy Melton, the opera singer and collector of antique cars. Mrs. Watson planned to drive it around town to save gasoline. We all took turns sitting in it and admiring the interior appointments, such as the small glass flower vase mounted on the side between the front and back seats. During the war years, Mrs. Watson could sometimes be seen driving her electric car down Madison Avenue to pick up Mr. Watson at the end of the day.

Seeing the Watsons' solicitude toward us I began to believe they felt a social responsibility towards those IBMers who had been uprooted from their families and friends. I appreciated their concern and always felt grateful to be included in any of their occasions. They always invited such interesting guests and the conversation invariably proved stimulating.

CHAPTER SEVEN

War Declared!

Sitting alone in my apartment on Sunday, December 7, 1941, two months after my arrival in New York, I panicked when I heard a radio announcer telling listeners the Japanese had bombed Pearl Harbor. According to his report, the West Coast could be the next target.

At first I couldn't believe what I'd heard. Then I grew frightened for my family in California. My frantic attempts to telephone them repeatedly met with busy signals, as all lines to the Coast were in use. So, I began calling Augusta, Jeanne Herman, and other Californians in New York to find out if they'd heard from their parents. The hours dragged on painfully, and like the others, I spent most of the night glued to my radio until I got through to my family. What a relief to hear their voices finally.

"We're O.K., Ruthie," my father reported. "But they're requiring us to have 'blackout' nights from now on. And tomorrow your mother and I plan to stock our shelves. Meanwhile, we keep our radio on all the time."

The office felt like a madhouse all that week. No one knew what projects to work on. With World War II escalating before our eyes and IBM personnel already leaving for active duty, Mr. Watson summoned me to his office.

"Miss Leach, I think you should go home for Christmas this year for a good visit with your family. These are trying times, and I am sure if I lived on the West Coast I would want to see my children as much as possible during wartime." Then he added, "While you are there, you might want to visit the West Coast offices, and on your way back, I'd like you to visit some other offices. We'll discuss them before you leave."

> *Dear Family—Don't know yet when I'll be home as I can't get in to see 'T.J.'...although Annie did and he asked her if I'd gone yet?! At least he's conscious of my going. With the present war crisis, I'll bet he'll forbid me from visiting Los Angeles...the most vital war spot next to Panama.*

Barrage balloons filled the sky over San Francisco Bay, greeting my train as we crossed the Carquinez Bridge near Oakland. The spooky scene drove home the realization that we truly were at war. That night my mother showed me their "blackout system" consisting of black shades at each window. The military required every resident of the San Francisco Bay area to observe the blackout so that should the enemy try to attack, no light could be seen from the air through the barrage balloons.

The government also rounded up our nice Japanese gardener, who had worked many years for my family, and shipped him, along with all the other West Coast Japanese to internment camps for the duration of the war. Travel, particularly at night, was limited, making life eerie under these circumstances. My father's company, the Hawaiian Pineapple Co. (Dole Pineapple), suffered losses because no shipments could come from Hawaii. Somehow, however, they coped with the times, as did others.

The Company Adapts

When I returned to New York the changes surprised me.

> *Dear Family—You should see the ground floor of the IBM building at 57th and Madison. The entire floor has been converted to a Red Cross Information Center. All day, they run a program to attract the public—concerts inside; in the window sculptors sculpting likenesses of such notables as*

*Swarthout, Lily Pons and others. All the activity disrupts
the traffic outside. War veterans play bingo with attractive
nurses on the corner. Someone else plays sick in bed in the
demonstration window. One day they had Clifton Webb
playing sick in bed!*

Eligible young men in IBM were joining the military in droves.
We had to revise our thinking about a working plan in the field
offices. Sales could only be made to companies engaged in war
work, so we cut sales quotas drastically, at the same time the
number of salesmen began to dwindle. We also had to reorganize
our factory work.

The first of my many "all-day" sessions in Mr. Watson's office
occurred in January 1942, shortly after my return from the West
Coast. He and I sat alone discussing my new job and a forthcom-
ing trip around the country. In the middle of our conversation, a
call came in from the Secretary of the Treasury, Henry
Morgenthau, in Washington. I fantasized listening in on something very important, but Mr. Watson quickly dismissed me and
asked me to return in about fifteen minutes. Darn it.

I returned with IBM's vice president Roy Stephens and
General Sales Manager Gordon Packard, to discuss the reorgani-
zation of the Endicott School.

"We need to remove the deadwood up at the school," Mr.
Watson pointed out. "Plus, we must rejuvenate the teaching staff
and the teaching manuals, as well. Has anyone looked at those
lately?"

Of course, I had. "I taught classes from the manuals last fall,
and you are right, they could stand some updating."

We discussed personalities at the school and the type of person
we should have there. We made various suggestions, then Mr.
Watson said, "I want to appoint you, Mr. Stephens, Mr. Packard,
and Miss Leach, as a committee of three to carry out the decisions
we made here this morning."

IBM never fired personnel except on moral grounds, such as
for lying, cheating, or committing some illegal act. So when Mr.
Watson formed a committee as a sort of "firing squad," he meant

for us to "promote" personnel to other jobs or give them "lateral" transfers, as we called them.

That morning proved exhausting for me, but I understood the school problem well, as I had spent the summer and fall teaching there. We also decided to have a systems service class the next month for all qualified women who were already working for IBM but who had not yet had the opportunity to attend classes in Endicott.

We all ate lunch in Mr. Watson's private dining room adjacent to his handsome walnut-paneled office. Another vice president, Charlie Kirk from Endicott, joined us, and we resumed our discussions about the school system, then worked out details for the new factory IBM was building to make guns for the war effort. I finally returned to my office at a quarter to four. What a different perspective of my job and the company I had now compared to even six months before.

Back at my desk, I suddenly realized I had a mere two weeks to prepare for the new systems service class—plan the curriculum, and sort out the logistics of who would attend, where we would house them, who would instruct them. What an enormous assignment to hand to this neophyte hardly dry behind the ears.

Somehow, though, I got the job done. By February 23rd, thirty young women from thirty IBM offices arrived in Endicott, representing all degrees of IBM knowledge and experience. Disparity made this class more difficult to teach than any class ever convened there.

Roy Stephens told me later, "Ruth, this class is solely your responsibility." The thought of running the show all by myself made my knees shake. In many ways, Mr. Watson's method of training executives was like teaching a child to swim by throwing her in the water. If you wanted to survive, you learned quickly, on the job. Oh well, I'd always been pretty good in the water.

CHAPTER EIGHT

IBM at War

Not long after the bombing of Pearl Harbor, IBM began noticing a dramatic change in staffing. When the Secretary of Education in Endicott, Charlie Love, left to join the Navy, Mr. Watson called me to his office and asked me to take over that position, since I had begun recruiting more personnel for Endicott training, anyway. I pleaded with him not to assign me permanently, as I wanted to keep my apartment in New York. So, as a compromise, he announced to the IBM family, "Miss Leach will now replace Mr. Love as head of the IBM School, in addition to her other duties."

So, instead of moving back to Endicott, I commuted from my New York City apartment. I soon found I needed some personal life aside from IBM, which, in Endicott, occupied my time day and night.

My duties, expanding almost too fast for me now, included teaching and overseeing more classes in Endicott as well as in field offices, where we trained an enormous number of armed forces personnel in the use of IBM machines. I became the Delaware Lackawanna Railroad's best commuter between New York and Binghamton (near Endicott) during those years.

Frustrated by the forced reduction in sales activity during the war, Mr. Watson began spending more time in Endicott than New

York. He loved to sell and had been designated America's Top Salesman by *Fortune* magazine and other publications of the time. But with IBM leasing new machines only to industries tied to the war effort, he had no new markets to conquer. So instead, he concentrated on education.

Made tense by this change, he would blow his top at the slightest provocation. The machine manuals must be updated, he insisted, and right away! I lost two of my best instructors that year thanks to all the extra assignments he gave us each time he tore the education department apart. Years later, we realized he was almost always right in the decisions he made. But the way he arrived at those decisions, like a (usually) benevolent dictator—ranting and raving and demanding that we do everything instantly—kept us all off balance. I always had trouble sleeping after one of those days. I often wondered if corporate life in other large companies was as volatile as ours.

> *Dear Family—T.J. has been here in Endicott for two weeks now and has worn everyone out. Where that man gets his energy I'm sure I don't know! He goes to bed late (3 a.m. this morning having inspected the night shift) and is always the first one at breakfast in the dining room the next morning. He's leaving Sunday, I hope!*

Training the Troops...in More Ways than One

Military installations across the country quickly expanded their use of IBM machines, as did war-related industries such as shipbuilding, aircraft plants, and others. Consequently, teaching at Endicott and systems service work in the field offices became very important to the war effort. By 1942, the systems service women pictured themselves as the "women behind the men behind the guns," and so they tackled every job enthusiastically. They taught military personnel how to use the machines and supervised new installations in wartime plants. As time went by, it became obvious we needed more systems service help.

During those years, each customer's lease of an IBM punched card accounting machine entitled him to maintenance services at IBM's expense. The salesman who sold an account oversaw the maintenance of all the machines, sending IBM customer engineers to insure that all customer employees were properly trained by a systems service person. But now, we began losing hundreds of salesmen to the military services.

In the spring of 1942, Mr. Watson called me in to discuss a replacement program. We no longer held sales contests or conventions. Only the needs of existing customers had to be taken care of, and their IBM machines maintained.

One day Mr. Watson said to me, "Now, Miss Leach, I want you to recruit the brightest young women graduates from the top colleges and universities—let's try for a hundred women. Then, train them in Endicott the way you were trained and assign them to the offices most in need of help."

"But, Mr. Watson," I said, "I've never interviewed college graduates for a job before. I wouldn't know where to start."

"Simply look for character and good manners, and we'll do the rest in Endicott."

Then I asked where he envisioned housing one hundred women in Endicott. He thought the Hotel Frederick would take care of them, but I had a bright idea.

"Mr. Watson, what would you think of using 'Tent City' since there won't be any convention up there this year?" The company built Tent City to house the men attending IBM's annual recognition event, the Hundred Percent Club. Situated just above the Homestead, the area held dozens of two-bed tents and well built spacious permanent latrines for every eight or so tents. A good cleaning and a few new boards would make it habitable once again.

Mr. Watson seemed dubious, but I pursued the idea. "I've had a lot of camping experience as a Camp Fire Girl in the Sierras, and if we present the idea to the students properly, I think they'll find the idea appealing." Eventually, I sold him.

With the help of IBM's district managers across the U.S., I mapped out the number of women needed in each district and the

colleges and universities in each area to visit. I asked the managers
to look over the graduating classes and line up likely prospects for
me to interview. I wanted young women in the top ten percent of
their class, preferably economics majors. I quoted to the managers
Mr. Watson's words to me, "Look for character and good manners,
and we'll do the rest in Endicott."

During my travels, I also recruited instructors for teaching in
Endicott from July to October. And the managers rarely seemed
happy about letting their best systems service women go for even
that short span of time.

So off I went, hitting a good nine or ten offices in a two-week
period. I traveled by plane when I could, but mostly I had to go by
train or even by bus when necessary. Massive troop movements
meant frequent delays on all forms of transportation. Invariably, I
caught a train with four or five cars of troops on it. I was often the
only woman on board, sometimes arriving at my destination in
the middle of the night.

> *Dear Family—I wish you could see the trains and planes*
> *these days. I'm usually the only female on a plane, but all*
> *the men are in uniform, as you might well know. It's fun to*
> *talk to them all…whoever sits next to me, I always strike*
> *up some conversation…and all the men I've encountered*
> *have been awfully nice young chaps. Uniforms are certain-*
> *ly standardizing and democratic things, aren't they? They*
> *make all the boys look clean-cut. I feel I'm doing my part—*
> *USO or something— when I chat with them while travel-*
> *ing, since I can't stay in one place long enough to do any-*
> *thing else!*

Prize Students and Pajama Parties

We had an exceptional class that summer of one hundred
women graduates from some ninety colleges and universities.
Most of the students had served as either president or vice president of their class or entire student body or had received straight

A's all through their college careers. As an introduction to their training in Endicott, I told the group, "I want to compliment each and every one of you on the outstanding records you achieved in your college years. Today, you embark on a different course of study, both intensive and extensive. You all finished at the top of your respective classes for the last four years, but don't worry if you fail to achieve that status in this school. You've never before faced the level of competition that awaits you here.

"We've told you that as a systems service woman your job includes handling some of our customers' accounts. Their needs must be satisfied, for a disgruntled customer can mean a loss of several thousand dollars if he chooses to return our equipment. It also can mean the loss of a valued customer and his future business. So, we will train you to protect the revenue of this business. You will be our unsung heroines."

Some of these prize students did have difficulty accepting that they no longer sat at the top of their class. I spent one night walking the golf course into the wee hours with a distraught student who even contemplated suicide. Another wanted to leave Endicott because she had received a "B" on a test. On the whole, though, they were an outstanding group who enjoyed fun and frolic after study hours.

Tent City worked beautifully until the end of August when the nights grew cooler. One of the girls from the South complained bitterly of the cold to Mr. Watson on one of his visits to Endicott. He then, of course, complained to me. I remembered at our camp in the Sierras we put newspapers under the mattresses to make the beds warmer, and we did that immediately. I also bought electric heaters for each tent.

We coaxed my roommate, Jane Parrish, a bugler, to rouse us happily in the early mornings with reveille, followed by snappy tunes, and then to end the day with Taps. Poor Jane had to sleep with her trumpet under her covers to keep it warm so it could perform properly on cold mornings.

I also instigated what I called "latrine parties," with each group taking a turn as "hostesses" near—but not too near—a numbered latrine at 9 p.m. on certain nights. They served hot chocolate, coffee, sodas, and cookies, or whatever they wanted. I tried desperately to make them all comfortable.

Not satisfied with my solution to the cool nights, Mr. Watson said to me one morning, "Miss Leach, I want you to go down to Macy's in New York City as soon as you can and order two pairs of 'Dr. Dentons' pajamas for each student. That will keep them warm. And Arch, you can accompany Miss Leach to the city for this purchase." Arch Davis, the IBM public relations officer who happened to be in Endicott on business, learned once again that sitting next to Mr. Watson at the wrong time could be dangerous. This wasn't the first time he'd been stuck with unwanted assignments thanks to his proximity to the boss.

Later, I saw Arch alone in the hall of the Homestead. "I'll meet you at the entrance to Macy's lingerie department tomorrow morning. Right now I have to spend a little time on the personal applications of this class to determine what size each girl wears. I'll take the sleeper down later."

When I met him the next morning, standing beside a black lace nightie at the entrance to the department, I asked, "Arch, have you ever been in a ladies' lingerie department before?" I thought not, judging from the color of his face and the nervous twitch he always developed when faced with anxious moments of any kind.

"Heavens, no, Ruth, I'll just let you go ahead and do the honors, if that's all right with you."

"But Arch, look at these ecstatic sales girls. They just know I'm your cutie, and you plan to buy me some expensive slinky number. When we ask to see some Dr. Dentons, they won't believe us. You don't want to miss their expressions then, do you?" Arch needed prodding to have a little fun, but in the end we had a great time hamming it up.

We found what we wanted, the cotton flannel one-piece pajamas with footies and a buttoned "back door." and handed the salesgirl an order for some two hundred pajamas in various sizes. As she busily wrote down the details, she suddenly asked, "Are you two running some kind of camp?"

In a quiet but steady voice I answered, "No, it's a business."

I'm sure we left her in a complete quandary, wondering what sort of monkey business we might be up to.

The next evening in Endicott the weather turned quite cold. In gratitude for their new nighties, the entire systems service class donned their new pajamas over their own clothing and paraded slowly in single file around the circular driveway in front of the Homestead entrance, each girl holding a lighted candle and singing a "Thank you, Mr. Watson" song they had composed themselves with Jane Parrish's help.

Mr. Watson watched from the door and felt so touched he invited the entire group into the dining room, pajamas and all, for hot chocolate and cookies to warm them up. Somehow, photographers appeared from nowhere, and bulbs flashed at our leader surrounded by a sea of Dr. Dentons. We all sang old songs, and everyone had a merry time—except me.

I suddenly felt very nervous about such a scene appearing on the front page of any newspaper, particularly IBM's. Mr. Watson would look ridiculous, and no one would believe the girls were fully clad in sweaters and wool slacks underneath their pajamas. So I forced myself to whisper in Mr. Watson's ear that we really should confiscate the films right then, for obvious reasons. For once he agreed with me, and I told Arch to take care of the photographers and their film. After a few more songs, the party ended.

Maintaining Morale

Three and a half months in Endicott without any social life made the young ladies somewhat cranky. During my days as a student there, we had dinners and dances and fun with the sales classes, but now we had an all-female class. Mr. Watson seemed aware of the problem, however, because he kept inviting his well-known friends to visit, such as Irene Dunne, who came up to Endicott and Binghamton to sell war bonds. For the price of a war bond, any one could attend the dinner we put on in her honor.

Earlier in the summer, opera stars Jimmy Melton and Lily Pons, both of whom stayed at the Homestead and ate their meals with the girls, also provided entertainment.

One morning, Mr. Watson had a farmer bring down a pair of oxen and a cart from the farm behind the Homestead to give Mr. Melton and Miss Pons a ride with some of the girls. Miss Pons handed me the pet Lhasa Apso she had brought with her and said, "Please, please take my baby for a long walk. She needs her exercise." I guess she considered me her personal maid.

The two stars had come up to sing at the dedication of the company's huge new factory addition built for making guns for the war effort. So, in spite of the lack of a social life, the girls always had some activity of interest going on to amuse them.

The sale of war bonds brought many celebrities to Broome County, one of the wealthiest counties in New York State. When they came, IBM usually housed and fed them at the Homestead, and our young ladies enjoyed dining with the likes of Bing Crosby, Bob Hope, Ogden Nash, and wonderful Gracie Fields, then the highest paid comedienne in the British Isles.

Bing, who put on a golf match for the war bond drive at the IBM golf course, practiced putting on the lawn in front of the Homestead, with our young ladies happily snapping photos of him. After the match he sang a few songs for the crowd: a big day in everyone's diary.

To help build employee loyalty to the company, Mr. Watson paid personal attention to each person. He'd picked up this method in Dayton, Ohio, when he worked for John H. Patterson, president of National Cash Register. The young ladies in that wartime class will probably never forget Mr. Watson for all the things he did for them during their stay in Endicott.

Class Finally Closes

After three extensions, the last week of this systems service class finally arrived. And it seemed far busier than I'd expected. Mr. and Mrs. Watson appeared again on a Monday with a delightful guest, Malvina Hoffman, a world-famous sculptress and a student of Rodin. Her sense of humor delighted us all, and we found her lecture and sculpture exhibit fascinating. Mr. Watson asked me to supervise the luncheon in her honor with Mrs. Watson presiding. Then he asked me to escort Miss Hoffman to and from her evening's lecture, held elsewhere.

Meanwhile, in my spare time (!) I interviewed all one hundred women in the class before their graduation that Wednesday. The transportation man at the railroad station failed me, so the job of handling tickets and baggage to eighty-one points of destination also fell in my lap. The graduation and dinner for five hundred that evening needed a seating list: who should sit on the dais, what VIPs had Mr. Watson invited at the last minute without telling anyone, and where did he want them seated?

Whatever speech I delivered that evening I made up at the dinner table. During the salad course, the lights went out all over the valley, putting everyone on edge. No one knew whether we'd had an air raid or what. We ate dinner by candlelight, but fortunately the electricity came back on during the speeches. Thank heavens we could all pack our clothes in Tent City that night without fumbling in the dark.

The graduation celebration lasted well into the early morning hours. I hoped we had successfully sent these bright, attractive young women on the IBM way, just as I had been sent on mine two and a half years before.

The next morning, we took the entire class down to New York for a quick visit to World Headquarters, then on to the Watson's home for an early dinner.

What a wild week I'd had, full of too many unexpected details. By the end of it, I was running on nervous energy and had an impressive set of dark circles under my eyes from carrying out my boss's orders. I despised the thought of turning into another "Watson lackey," without adding any creativity of my own to my job. But the war and all the patriotism of the times spurred all of us on to do whatever we had to do. Plus, I actually enjoyed life in Endicott. Where else would I meet such interesting people and make a comparable contribution to the war effort? The only problem—eating and sleeping IBM twenty-four hours a day without any respite.

CHAPTER NINE

Giving Our All

In the following summers, many other classes for systems service women occupied Tent City. We also held smaller classes in the winter months, but housed the students elsewhere. Although we trained hundreds of women during the war years, we couldn't do it fast enough. By 1943, the government regularly hired our women away from us as fast as we could train them. The WAVES, the WACS, government installations of IBM equipment necessary to the war effort, and even the Red Cross overseas operations, all made glamorous appeals to our systems service women. Since IBM had pledged all of its facilities, including some personnel, to the U.S. Government for the war effort, we gave the women our blessings as they left, even though their departure left a void in our own ranks.

Our customer engineers also began leaving for the military at an alarming rate. These men from the field offices maintained the IBM customers' accounting machines. Already, we had been training women in Rochester, New York to handle the maintenance on IBM electric typewriters, so we hired seventy-nine more young women to train as customer engineers on the accounting machines. They graduated in the fall of 1943, and we sent them out, screwdrivers in hand, to work alongside the remaining engineers in the field offices.

IBM converted the Endicott factory one hundred percent to the war effort, producing all kinds of equipment for the armed forces—bombsights, carbines, automatic rifles, cannons, gun directors, and fire control mechanisms, as well as punched card machines of pre-war design. IBM engineers also undertook about one hundred special development projects for the armed forces. We even bought a small house in Endicott, decorated it and furnished it just for all the Army and Navy personnel to stay in when they came on business to our factory or engineering laboratory.

The company often called upon me to escort these high-ranking men through the factory, the engineering lab, and the IBM School. One of these men, General Follett Bradley of the Army Air Corps, had been Tom Watson Jr.'s boss during his years in the Air Force.

Another visitor, General William S. Knudsen, former president of General Motors, headed the U.S. War Production Board, which organized all factory production of war products in the country. The company deemed the general's visit to Endicott so important that Mr. Watson personally escorted him to inspect our factory work.

During this inspection, I received a phone call at the school from across the street. Mr. Watson said casually, "Miss Leach, please gather all the classes you have over there in our largest room for a reception and a talk by the general. And, by the way, I would like you to introduce him to the group. We'll be there in about fifteen minutes."

He hung up before I could ask him for facts about the general, some crumb of information to help me introduce him properly. I knew almost nothing about the man. Furthermore, we needed more than fifteen minutes to remove the partitions and make three rooms into one, get the classes together, bring in a lectern and a microphone, call the photographer and the stenotypist to take notes, and set up chairs. Did Mr. Watson consider me a magician?

The whole school pitched in and helped me set up. I had just picked up a long pointer off the floor when the visiting firemen walked in the door. In fact, I nearly poked General Knudsen in the stomach with the pointer.

"We're almost ready, sir. We must test the microphone, then

we'll be ready." I stalled, hoping to find someone in the group who might tell me something about the general, but Mr. Watson insisted I get along with my introduction.

At the lectern I drew a blank. Was he a general at General Electric or General Motors? Hmmm...

"Ladies and gentlemen," I started, "we have, indeed, a surprise for you this morning. General William S. Knudsen joins us here today to make an inspection of our factory and engineering lab on behalf of the War Production Board, of which he is the head. Many of you have seen his picture in pre-war newspapers and magazines as president of er- er- General Electric, I mean General Motors. So it is my pleasure to introduce General Knudsen who will say a few words to you at this time. General Knudsen."

The whole fiasco flustered me so I had difficulty understanding the General with his thick Danish accent. In fact, I had no idea what he'd said. I knew I had to comment on his speech when he sat down. Most hosts at the time thanked speakers for their "pearls of wisdom," weaving in some of the thoughts that the speakers had just expressed. When General Knudsen finished, I drew a blank for the second time. So I said, "Thank you, general, for all of the pearls of wisdom you have shared with us today. We appreciate your stopping by to see us...Mr. Watson, do you have a word or two for us at this time?" Of course he did.

Dear Family—What a week this has been! Talk about celebrities. General Knudsen arrived Tuesday morning by bomber accompanied by colonels, majors, captains, the Air Corps, State troopers, flags, motorcycles, etc. When he came to address my students, T.J. introduced me to him, and then I found myself on the platform with the General on my right, T.J. on my left, and colonels & majors down the line. After I finished saying something into the microphone, I know not what right now, I turned to sit down. As I did, my chair hit the chair next to it, which hit the flag pole, which proceeded to fall over and klonk me on the head! Such was the General's visit to the schoolhouse.

Working for Mr. Watson wasn't easy. He often called on me to perform duties like that impromptu speech when I really didn't have the information required to do the job right. Maybe he considered that part of a plan for career development, another learning experience. I, however, called it "putting me on the spot when I least expected it."

Wartime in New York

During the war years, everyone talked at great length about the rationing of gas, food, clothing, and many other items by the National Ration Board. Transportation was such a big issue that in New York, where almost everyone had access to public transportation, people considered you unpatriotic if you drove your own car. So walking the streets one saw nothing but buses and taxicabs and, of course, Mrs. Watson in her electric car.

Food stamps, vital to every household, were used sparingly, and served as a topic of conversation everywhere. Because of shortages, meat lovers learned to like pasta more than they really wanted to. Sometimes we exchanged our ration coupons with our families far away or pooled them with others to get the items we wanted and needed. The ration board allowed each person only three pairs of shoes a year, so I sent some of my shoe coupons to my sister for her growing children, and I sent sugar coupons to my mother.

One particular evening, my roommate Mary Lou and I had decided to pool our coupons and throw a small dinner party for friends. Earlier that day, however, a casual friend invited me to a cocktail party that same evening at a much-talked-about brownstone in the East Sixties. This friend, a public relations man, catered to the rich and famous and the party was being held at the home of Sherman Fairchild, of Fairchild Aviation fame. Mr. Fairchild had remodeled the house for himself and his aunt, who had lived with him for a number of years. The refurbished house proved so unusual that several papers and magazines had featured its unusual design in articles. Instead of stairways, ramps led from the first floor to the fifth, with an atrium of green-dyed gravel in the center, opening to the sky and planted with orange and lemon trees. Everyone in Manhattan wished for a look inside, so I grabbed the opportunity. I even asked my new roommate, Mary Lou, to come along with us.

Sherman Fairchild, the son of one of IBM's first stockholders, was himself a member of the IBM Board, having inherited his father's stock. He had planned this fancy party to entertain his aviation friend, Howard Hughes. As soon as Mary Lou and I entered in our "Kitty Foyle" suits of navy blue with white collars and cuffs, I felt immediately out of place. Sherman's surprise and, I think, embarrassment at seeing me didn't help, either.

Twin pianos and a bevy of "beauties" filled the living room. By the looks of our surroundings, Sherman had called up a glitzy model agency and told them to send over an equal number of blondes and brunettes with a smattering of redheads, all dressed to the teeth in glitter, cleavage, plastic high heeled shoes and sprayed pompadour hairdos—the type of models who work mostly at night.

To extricate myself from this scene, I asked a waiter where I could find a telephone. I had just remembered our neighborhood grocery store closed at 6 p.m., and I wanted the butcher to leave our precious hamburger at the bakery next door for me to pick up. So I trotted up the first ramp to the library...only to find it occupied by a man dressed in old jeans and dirty sneakers, with long stringy hair. Could this be another misfit like myself? When he turned toward me, I recognized our guest of honor, Howard Hughes.

"Pardon me, sir, but do you see a telephone in this room?"

"I've been looking for the phone, too," he replied, "but I can't find it. I've got to call Hollywood. Our host is such an inventor, he probably has it hidden somewhere, and it won't appear till we push the right button."

"Well," I said, "why don't you take that side of the room and I'll take this side, and we'll look for a button to push. I've got to call my butcher before 6 p.m. I'm having a dinner party tonight, and I've got to pick up some hamburger with my last food stamps for the month. Don't you hate to part with your food stamps?"

I chattered on nervously in a one-sided conversation. What did Howard Hughes know about such mundane things as food stamps and hamburger? Then, as he pressed a button on a table top, a panel slid back and up came the phone.

"Now you can make your call and get your hamburger."

"Oh, no, you were up here first, so you go ahead and make your call." Of course, I wanted to hear what he had to say to Hollywood. I just knew that conversation would be more interesting to my guests than my hamburger casserole. But he politely insisted, "Ladies before gentlemen."

When I returned to the living room, I found Mary Lou in the middle of the fancy ladies, asking them where they had their hair done, where one found those pretty plastic see-through handbags, and so on. I hated to ruin her fun, but told her the time had come for us to go part with some food stamps. We said goodbye to our host, and our escort. I'm sure he preferred glitz to Kitty Foyle, anyway. We left before Mr. Hughes finished his call, and giggled all the way home.

Moving Again

In September of 1943, a depressing message awaited my return to New York City from Endicott. The owner of my beautiful Sutton Place apartment wanted it back by November first. I had lost my roommate, who returned to California when her job was curtailed by the war, and my next roommate, one of my instructors in Endicott, lasted only a few months before she left to marry a naval officer.

After a long, frustrating search, I finally settled alone in a dark unfurnished studio at 51st Street and Second Avenue. Living with orange crates for tables and chairs until I could buy some furniture, I felt pretty sorry for myself. The studio, located on the second floor, looked out over a fire escape in the back, and I could see only a slice of sky pinched between two buildings...definitely no Sutton Place.

Not long after I moved in, in an apartment down the street, a man murdered his wife and escaped down a fire escape. Every time I looked out my window and saw my own fire escape, I became uneasy. I decided I just couldn't live there another minute. Eventually, I found a lovely furnished place up on 79th, around the corner from the Metropolitan Museum, and I let Mona and Karl Malden have the 51st Street studio for the duration of my lease.

CHAPTER TEN

Wartime and Mr. Watson

During these years, every day seemed to bring a new fund drive or benefit program for some war effort or other. Mr. Watson insisted that IBM always take at least one table at such functions, which usually took place at the Waldorf Astoria. He really wanted the IBM name before the public at all costs and he wanted to show that we were behind the war effort one hundred percent.

If our president sat on the dais, we IBMers at the table observed very carefully who sat next to him, as we knew it would have a direct bearing on our future. Invariably Mr. Watson would question his seat mate about the most difficult job he had to perform in his office.

Once, I was told, at a luncheon before the war, he sat next to a banker, who told Mr. Watson that his most difficult job was sorting the incoming daily checks according to the banks on which they were drawn. After consulting with IBM engineers, Mr. Watson came up with the bankproof machine, quite an innovation in the banking world at the time. I remember demonstrating that machine at the San Francisco Fair before scores of people and praying they would not ask me any detailed questions about banking operations, since the extent of my banking knowledge was how to run the machine.

At one Waldorf luncheon during the war, Mr. Watson sat next to U.S. Navy Commander Howard H. Aiken. Back in 1937, when he was a graduate student in physics at Harvard University, Aiken had come up with the idea of coupling together a series of control mechanisms to accommodate long sequences of operations. He pursued this project when he became head of the mathematics department at Harvard, where the Navy was conducting top secret research. In fact, Aiken had contacted IBM about building such a machine when the war intervened. With Aiken called to active duty in the Navy, and IBM geared to produce war equipment, Aiken's project got put on the back burner for the time being.

From my position at the IBM table I thought I could tell when Mr. Watson was asking his usual question of the commander. I soon learned that in reply, Commander Aiken told him about the enormously complex mathematical problems he was now working on for the Navy.

I remember, too, the usual meeting in Mr. Watson's office following the Waldorf luncheon, with Clair Lake, IBM's chief engineer, and his engineering staff present.

"Mr. Lake, you have had discussions with Commander Aiken before about his project, though it was some time ago. Now I want you to give priority to Aiken's original idea, to come up with a machine to handle the difficult computations the commander is now doing. As you know, this is so very important to the war effort."

Several months later, the efforts of our engineers resulted in the Mark I, which Clair built in the engineering lab in Endicott and demonstrated to the Harvard faculty in December 1943. Eventually, the machine was dismantled and sent to Harvard to be reassembled. Named the IBM Automatic Sequence Controlled Calculator, the company formally presented it to the university on August 7, 1944.

Periodically, on my visits to the engineering lab in Endicott, I would stop by Clair Lake's lab to check up on his progress. "Clair, how many electromechanical cams and relays have you built into your machine today?" I teased.

He smiled and said, "Now Ruth, do you really want me to count all of them just for you?"

Then I asked him, "What are you going to do when you get to

the end of this room and you still have more cams and relays to go?"

"Well, I guess I'll have to tear down the wall into the next room." And he did just that before the 51-feet-long, 8-feet-high machine was finally finished.

After fifteen years of service at Harvard, a portion of this first Automatic Sequence Control Calculator went to rest at the Smithsonian Institution in Washington DC. The introduction of crystal diodes and, later, in the early '50s, transistors into research and development programs allowed IBM to produce a much faster machine after the war ended.

Towards the close of the war at still another Waldorf luncheon, Mr. Watson sat on the dais next to Harold Russell, a well-known war hero who had lost both his hands and who later appeared in the film "The Best Years Of Our Lives," for which he received an Academy Award. Mr. Watson became so intrigued with this man's dexterity that he brought him down to the IBM table and introduced him to us.

"Mr. Russell, will you show my IBM friends here how you use your hooks for hands?" Russell lit a cigarette for us and demonstrated how he manipulated a knife and fork. Not only did he impress me with his ability to handle himself, but I also found his upbeat, positive personality extremely attractive.

Again, immediately following that luncheon, Mr. Watson called a meeting in his office.

"Can any of you imagine going through the rest of your life with hooks like Mr. Russell's, in place of hands? I brought him down to the table to show you how he dealt with the situation. Now, why can't we come up with something better? Why can't we devise something that resembles a real hand and operates in some way like a real hand does? We make war products for the war effort. Why shouldn't we help our injured veterans lead more normal lives?"

The next thing I knew, we were in the prosthesis business, creating devices that emulated a human hand, actuated by little motors at the elbow with no forearm, or motors wired to the foot if the whole arm was lost.

We hired a nice young veteran who had lost both arms early in the war, one arm below the elbow and the other, above the elbow. He graciously served as our guinea pig. Mr. Watson appointed me as the IBM liaison with the U.S. Army medical group on this project, and I worked with our veteran, helping him practice the various assignments I gave him, such as grabbing a single sheet of paper out of the bottom drawer of a desk and putting it in a typewriter; or taking a spoon, putting a single egg in it and carrying it to the other side of the room; and using a knife and fork to cut a piece of meat.

After several weeks passed, a delegation from the U.S. Army medical group came to review his progress. He passed their inspection with flying colors and they transferred him back to the Army medical group for further tests and studies. At that point, the project was put under their jurisdiction. I felt proud of the record this young man made and proud of our engineers who contributed so much to the lives of our injured veterans.

I have often wondered if others knew what an incredibly driven man Mr. Watson was, so inquisitive, and with such boundless energy. Sometimes I found it exhausting just working for him...always having to run just to keep up.

Following Our Leader

As the war went on, the group of top executives that Mr. Watson depended on in daily discussions in his office began to thin out due to illnesses, deaths, and transfers to the military and other jobs. I became one of the newcomers he turned to, and I found myself given more responsibility, despite my inexperience. For example, what did I know about prostheses before I got the job of following through on making an artificial hand?

With so much going on in my department and the request to hire more women for another systems service school, I had to get some help. Mr. Watson, at my suggestion, appointed Mary Schultz from the original systems service class of 1935 and a mainstay of the Newark, New Jersey, office. Mary transferred to World Headquarters as head of personnel in 1942, and four months later became assistant systems service manager. There, her superb administrative abilities and dedication to detail blossomed.

She and I started out by sharing an office, since we were both so busy, traveling in opposite directions to hire more college graduates for the upcoming classes in Endicott. We also carried out other assignments that came our way from "upstairs" (Mr. Watson's office), many of which proved most unusual, too.

One day in 1942, Mary and I received a summons to Mr. Watson's office. "Ladies," he said, "I want you to meet Mme. Ignez D'Araujo, Brazil's only woman diplomat in her country's foreign service. President Vargas of Brazil sent her to me as she is seeking something in our educational institutions that she could adapt to her country."

Mr. Watson obviously had no idea how to solve her problem, and after discussions with her in fractured English, none of us could figure out exactly what she was after. Mr. Watson then picked up the phone and made an appointment for her to see President Conant of Harvard. He assigned Mary and me to escort her to Cambridge, Massachusetts, hoping she might find what she sought in our universities.

Like many things Mr. Watson planned, this trip proved far more difficult than it sounded. For one thing, Mr. Watson decided to send Mike Supa with us, a blind, physically handicapped IBM employee recently promoted to World Headquarters from Endicott. Also along for the trip was Mr. Clemmons, my former boss in Atlanta, now with the education department in Endicott. What a strange group to organize for a wartime trip to Boston. One of us would lead Mike, with his white cane, while another would hold onto Mme. D'Araujo's arm at all times. Though a charming lady, her lack of English coupled with our lack of Portuguese made the journey a challenge.

Healthy and hardy Americans had trouble enough with public transportation during the war. Imagine how difficult it could be for a blind person and one who spoke little of the native tongue. We really needed a five-passenger car or limo with a chauffeur who knew where to go, since none of us knew Boston. Civilians couldn't get limos during the war, but luckily, since we were escorting a Brazilian diplomat, we got permission to have a car.

After spending two full days attending Harvard's labor seminars along with members of the C.I.O and the Longshoremen's Union, Mme. D'Araujo decided this was not what she wanted, nor could President Conant help her any further. So poor was her English that she could not make her needs understood.

Belatedly, I suggested calling on the Brazilian Consulate where someone might help us interpret her requests.

Voila! As it turned out, she wasn't looking for educational programs at all, but rather a school for citizenship. Many Europeans had escaped their wartorn countries and settled in Brazil, which had no official program to orient these refugees to the customs and laws of their new country. Madame was simply searching for a model she could use to help her create such a program. The assistant Consul-General, Señor Lopez, suggested we go to Syracuse University and look into their Maxwell School of Citizenship.

"Señor Lopez," I asked, "did you by any chance attend U.C. Berkeley?" Slowly, recognition dawned on him. "Of course! You sat next to me in classes where we were seated alphabetically. After all these years, what a surprise." He helped us tremendously, and we felt forever indebted to him for solving the problem for Mme. D'Araujo.

It goes to show how blindly we followed Mr. Watson sometimes. One of us should have thought about consulting the Brazilian Consulate in New York before we wasted a week and a half of our time, to say nothing of Mme. D'Araujo's and Dr. Conant's time. We expected Mr. Watson to think of everything because he usually did.

We introduced Mme. D'Araujo to Syracuse University's Chancellor Tolley, whom I knew from his frequent appearances at IBM graduations and he eagerly agreed to help. After spending a couple of days attending classes in the school of citizenship at Syracuse, at last our Brazilian diplomat found what she wanted.

Although the whole tour felt like a wild goose chase, I did enjoy meeting Mme. D'Araujo, a real character.

Dear Family—What a tour this has been! Mme. D'Araujo is as interesting a character as I've ever met…about 48 years old and the mother of a 27-year-old daughter. She told me her husband was unfaithful…"eet" made her "too seeeeck." So she separated from him. Apparently in South America it's accepted for the men folk to have more than one love. But her husband did not have good enough taste in other women to suit Madame.

Once the trip ended, I also realized how much I had enjoyed spending time with Mike Supa, my blind friend. He made me realize how those of us with sight can actually be blind. The simple things of life that we all take for granted were such pleasures to him.

All in a Day's Work

On another occasion Mr. Watson asked Mary Schultz and me to accompany him to Poughkeepsie along with the IBM vice president of manufacturing from Endicott, Charlie Kirk, and Roy Stephens, vice president at World Headquarters in New York City. IBM had purchased a building in 1941 on the Hudson River near Poughkeepsie, primarily to set up a subsidiary gun-manufacturing company. The War Department had contracted with IBM back in 1940 to set up a plant of this sort. Since Mr. Watson felt reluctant to turn his beloved Endicott plant into a munitions factory, he thought he could divorce this work from IBM machines manufacturing in Endicott by setting up the gun factory in Poughkeepsie. By 1943, with the U.S. at war, Mr. Watson changed his tune; he went all out for war work in every IBM factory.

Before lunch on that day, he organized a planning session to brainstorm ways to make this Poughkeepsie factory setup as good as the one in Endicott.

"Particularly," Mr. Watson said, "I want to emphasize the facilities of our women employees, as I am sure we are going to employ many more women than we ever have before.

"Also," he continued, "we must build a country club for all of our employees on the order of the one in Endicott, complete with a golf course."

After lunch he escorted the four of us to a large piece of property with rolling hills that he had just purchased, adjacent to the IBM plant. He wanted our opinions on where to build the country club and 18-hole golf course. We all enjoyed playing architect that day, first planning a new addition to the plant and then building a country club and a golf course—as if we had any idea what we were doing.

Mary and I had worn our best suits, silk stockings and high heeled shoes (at a premium in war time), not realizing we would be climbing banks of earth and wading through tall grass and weeds galore. Two pairs of silk stockings and two pairs of good shoes bit the dust in more ways than one that afternoon. I felt furious with Mr. Watson for dragging us over hill and dale with no warning.

Mr. Watson, in an expansive mood during our walk, waved his arms as he mentally placed each green on the course. I quietly giggled to myself as I counted those waves he made. I figured each wave of his hand would cost at least $3000 (1943 prices), and I prayed he would have the sense to employ a real golf course architect to lay out a decent course and not take any suggestions from the four of us or try to do it himself. I am sure he did, but I never got into golf course planning again.

On still another trip, this time to Rochester, NY, with Mr. and Mrs. Watson, Mary, and Loraine MacLennan, a systems service district manager, we toured the IBM typewriter plant of about 800 factory workers, where classes were held for training women to service IBM electric typewriters. On the spur of the moment, the manager assembled all the factory workers and students to hear Mr. Watson speak. Then, in his frustratingly spontaneous way, he decided to introduce me to the group to say a few words.

Speechless, per usual, I stood wondering in those very few seconds of his introduction what on earth I could come up with to say to a factory group. Without thinking, I blurted out, "Well, as Antony said to Cleopatra upon entering her bedchamber, 'I didn't come here to talk!" The crowd roared, as I groped for a follow-up.

I had some interviewing to do in Rochester, later that day, so Mr. and Mrs. Watson returned to the hotel with Mary and Loraine. On passing a quality dress shop in the hotel entry, Mr. Watson said to his wife, "Jeannette, why don't you take the ladies inside and buy them each a nice suit." This thoughtfulness meant a great deal to my friends, as the government had frozen all of our salaries by that time. When I returned to the hotel and heard of the shopping spree, I said, "Gosh, I would have been happy with just a pair of new shoes to replace the ones I ruined in Poughkeepsie."

Later, when I read the biography of John H. Patterson, head of National Cash Register, I realized how many little ideas Mr. Watson copied from his former employer to endear his salesmen to their company. Often Mr. Patterson took a salesman or two to New York with him on business and while there would buy them each a new suit. That personal attention would motivate them to work that much harder in their jobs. It certainly motivated Mary and Loraine.

Spending so much time in Mr. Watson's office gave me a chance to try and analyze the way he worked as a leader. After all, he built IBM, nurtured it and made it grow by attracting men and, later, women with character and good manners. He taught them salesmanship and all the other qualities he had learned from his own experience. He insisted on neat appearances, white collars and pressed suits. He expected the same from women employees when he began to hire them to replace the men in sales; we had to be neatly dressed at all times, complete with hat and gloves. Even in summertime, we wore stockings over our tanned legs.

Mr. Watson must have realized his thinking processes sharpened when he discussed ideas and problems of the business before an audience. Whoever sat in the "group," and I was usually the only woman, would then get an assignment to go to Newark to settle "that" problem or to Scranton to settle "this" one. Like poor Arch Davis, who I mentioned earlier. He had the misfortune to be sitting next to Mr. Watson in Endicott when he bellowed at me for not keeping my students warm enough and ordered Arch to accompany me to Macy's to buy Dr. Dentons. I could discern no real reason behind these assignments other than to expose some-one to another experience; Mr. Watson liked to "season" employ-ees. But Arch's visit to the lingerie department wasn't meant to broaden his perspective; I never did know whether Mr. Watson wanted me to have company or if he took his annoyance out on Arch.

In the case of Mike Supra, the blind employee Mr. Watson had us take along on our wild Brazilian goose chase to Harvard, he may have wanted Mme. D'Araujo to tell the world that IBM was one of the few corporations who hired physically handicapped people. Mr. Watson was an early master of public relations.

We never knew when an unusual task or assignment would fall into our laps. Once he summoned me upstairs to his office and asked me to sit in the chair at the right side of his desk. This would be a friendly conversation, I knew. Had he asked me to sit in the chair on the other side of his desk, the conversation might not have been so pleasant. I saw he had nothing on his desk except the current issue of *Think* magazine, the monthly publication for IBMers and customers. And I hadn't read it yet!

Mr. Watson smiled and handed me the magazine. "Miss Leach, I want you to criticize it."

I knew I had to say something, but what? After flipping through the pages I finally thought of comparing it to the easy-to-read *Reader's Digest*.

"Why not," I said, "complete an article before starting anoth-er? There's no advertising in this magazine, so there's no reason to continue a story on a back page. As it is now, Mr. Watson, the first few pages have photographs related to each article, and the rest of the issue is boring."

He said nothing, and I thought I had laid an egg. But no, he pressed a button to summon *Think* editor, Major Edmund Hackett, and his entire staff to the office immediately.

When they all assembled, Mr. Watson said, "We have been dis-cussing the format of your magazine, and we think the way it is now, with all the pictures in the first few pages only, is boring. Why not complete one article before starting another so that the visual interest provided by the photographs is distributed evenly throughout? Let's try it with the next issue, Major Hackett."

Mr. Hackett was aghast at this revolutionary idea, and said to Mr. Watson, "But we can't implement that idea now for the next issue. The presses are rolling at this very moment."

Our leader then stamped his foot and raised his voice to a shout, "Well then, stop the presses NOW! Why didn't YOU think of Miss Leach's idea on improving its appearance?"

His dramatic approach did get the results he wanted, but I shrank lower in my chair while Major Hackett's glaring eyes sent daggers towards me. For some fifty years, until its demise in 1993, *Think* magazine retained this format.

CHAPTER ELEVEN

Climbing the Corporate Ladder

One morning during the first week of November 1943, I received a summons to Mr. Watson's office.

"Miss Leach, I want to discuss an important matter with you. I think this company needs a 'Women's Division.' Our factories are full of women who have replaced the men who have gone to war. Plus, you have been hiring more young women to train in Endicott for work in the field offices." He looked pleased with himself. "What do you think of that idea?"

I couldn't believe what I'd heard. "What would a Women's Division accomplish that isn't being done now?" I asked him. "Why separate the ewes from the rams?" I could see he hadn't expected dissent.

"In wartime particularly," I told him, "if there were a job to be done in the company, I would put the best person in charge of that job, whether it be a man or a woman." I wanted him to understand why I opposed the whole idea.

I returned to the office I shared with Mary Schultz and found her sitting at her desk. I told her about the discussion upstairs, since we worked closely together in the hiring program and personnel training.

"Well, I agree with you," she said. "I'm strongly opposed to this division of work—I see no earthly reason for the separation."

The following Monday morning, November 11th to be exact, I again received a call to report to Mr. Watson's office.

"I am going ahead with plans for a Women's Division for our company, Miss Leach, and I want to promote you to be in charge of it."

Well, I thought, how am I going to get out of this?

"Mr. Watson, I'm always grateful when you promote me to greater heights in this business. But I honestly cannot accept the assignment because I don't believe in the whole concept." And so I declined the offer. He said he was sorry I felt the way I did, and I left his office.

On Wednesday, November 13th of that same week, I again got a summons to his office (one floor up from mine), where I found two vice presidents, Mr. Nichol and Mr. Stephens, sitting on either side of Mr. Watson.

He began by saying, "Miss Leach, since you disliked the idea of a Women's Division, I am offering you another position, that of assistant vice president of IBM. I have said before that you have excelled in hiring top women and training them well for systems service work. All your young women do such a great job for our country in servicing the wartime installations, as well as for IBM, and you should be rewarded for what you have done for our company."

I looked at Fred Nichol who had been with Mr. Watson for some twenty-five years, and then I looked at Roy Stephens, who had also been with the company for almost that long. To me, they always seemed like "yes" men to their boss, who relied on them to carry out his decisions. Would I then be another "yes" man? I wasn't sure where I would fit into this picture...those two with so many years of experience and me with only four years behind me. Besides, I had just turned twenty-seven, and they were at least thirty-to-thirty-five years older than I was.

Then I thought about what Mr. Watson had just talked about, and finally understood the big picture he was trying to paint. He wanted to emphasize and acknowledge the role of women, who were taking on increased responsibilities during the war effort, and I could buy into that reasoning. I believed he chose me largely because I was in the right place at the right time...but I didn't mind.

I knew I had matured on the job, having carried out my responsibilities that year right along with the rest of the senior executives at World Headquarters. Mr. Watson had certainly treated me as one of them. So I accepted this great challenge with the usual appreciation.

"It will be a pleasure to have you aboard, Miss Leach, in your new capacity. Now when you return to your office, please tell Miss Schultz I want to see her?" We all shook hands, with the other two V.P.s echoing their boss's felicitations.

When Mary returned to our office, she had a sour look on her face. "I'm just furious. I've just been assigned to head the Women's Division, and as you well know, I dislike the idea as much as you do. Now what happened to you upstairs?"

"Oh, now I'm to be an assistant vice president!" I answered. We both laughed, and seriously thought our promotions ludicrous. I said, "I wonder what new assignments tomorrow will bring?"

Friday, November 15th of this same famous week, I once again made the trip upstairs. Mr. Watson smiled. At least he was in a good mood. He then said, "Well, Miss Leach, we had a board of directors meeting this morning, and they elected you a full corporate vice president of IBM! So, my congratulations to you for a job well done."

I replied formally, as befitted my newly elevated stature. Besides, it didn't seem right to talk to Mr. Watson any other way.

"As I said last Wednesday, Mr. Watson, I have to thank you again for spearheading this particular honor through your board. I think you know how grateful I am for all the opportunities that have come my way, and I accept the board's decision on behalf of all the women in IBM. It is they who have done an outstanding job."

Then I asked as I turned to leave, "Shall I send Miss Schultz up to see you?"

He smiled and said, "Yes, please."

Mary then became assistant vice president. This time she returned all smiles. It had been a big week for both of us, and the subject of a "women's division" never surfaced again.

I burned up the phone wires to my parents in California that week, calling after each exciting announcement. After my third call, my father said, "What on earth is going on back there? Well, Ruthie, you've fooled them this far, you might as well fool them some more!" He never could understand how I could teach those machines or teach accounting principles when I'd flunked economics in college and failed business school, too. Mary and I continued to feel amazed by the week's happenings. Our phones rang off their hooks, with people calling from throughout the company.

> *Dear Family—Well—you have no idea what we have gone through, having spent practically one whole week in T.J.'s office trying to keep his idea under control. I certainly am not the type to push Women in Business, nor do I want to, but I tried my best to be so non-aggressive and then I come out at the end of the week with a job so huge in scope that I can't comprehend it at all.*

The following Monday morning, November 18, 1943, pictures of Mary Schultz and Ruth Leach were on the front pages of the financial sections of the *New York Times, The Washington Post, The New York Herald Tribune*, the *Wall Street Journal*, and other newspapers across the country. *The Oakland Tribune,* my hometown paper, spread a high school picture of me across its front page with a caption: LOCAL GIRL MAKES GOOD!

Though the promotion and all the fuss pleased me, I didn't feel any different inside, as I told my family in a letter home.

> *Many thanks Mommie, Daddy, Amie, Helen and Petie for your letters of congratulations—rest assured I still feel and act the same way I always have. I may have a change of title, but to me setting up a personnel file on every female in the business is just another systems service job!!*

Frankly, I hated to think what my fellow employees thought about Mary's and my appointments, particularly those older men who might have aspired to being a vice president one day themselves. They had families to support and were getting on in years. When the news broke, I longed to be a mouse under a desk in some big IBM office where I could judge the reaction.

I went to Washington that weekend so that on Monday morning I could sit in an obscure corner of the IBM office there in time to watch everyone come to work. Surprisingly, during that day, I felt the true warmth of everyone's congratulations, especially the older salesmen.

The national reaction made it clear that our appointments represented a public relations coup, which, of course, fit Mr. Watson's agenda perfectly. His announcement to the papers stated, "The appointments of Miss Leach and Miss Schultz are in keeping with the increased responsibilities women are assuming now in our defense factories and in the business world."

Though way ahead of his time, Mr. Watson knew just what he was doing by promoting women at IBM. But I cringed a little inside, wondering how I could handle this big assignment. I recognized that Mr. Watson always pushed everyone beyond what they thought they could do, sometimes with disastrous results.

In Demand

As the first woman vice president of a top corporation, I was suddenly in great demand as a speaker, and I had never made a major speech of any kind before. Within two weeks, I received an invitation to speak before the Second War Congress of American Industry held by the National Association of Manufacturers.

"I can't possibly speak before an audience of corporate heads and CEOs," I told Mr. Watson and Mr. Nichol. "I'm going to decline."

"Oh, you can't, Miss Leach, absolutely not!" Mr. Watson gasped.

"Why, this is our golden opportunity!" added Mr. Nichol.

"But what will I say?" I asked. "I have no facts, no figures, not even an opening joke."

"We'll help you write it," promised Mr. Watson, "and Mr. Nichol, who gives great speeches, will teach you the fine points of delivery. I am sure he can find you a good joke to start with, too."

How could I refuse the opportunity to have the two top executives of IBM working for me for a couple of weeks?

So the terrible morning arrived and I faced it blue with fright, after rehearsing my talk the entire night before. I just knew I'd fail miserably, and I had practiced my opening joke so many times that it no longer seemed funny. If the joke failed to relax the audience or me, I'd feel like a fool up there at the podium.

Sitting on the stage of the Waldorf-Astoria Ballroom that unforgettable moment, as the master of ceremonies introduced me, I realized that twenty-five hundred pairs of eyes would soon be focused on me, and several sets of those eyes belonged to my buddies from World Headquarters. I definitely felt stress with a capital S.

I began my speech with Mr. Nichol's joke, and because it was almost too feminist for the year 1943, I quote it here:

"Because my position here is somewhat unusual, I should like to tell you a story. About the time of World War I, when agitation for adoption of women's suffrage was at its peak, a young suffragette joined up with an old-timer in the hazardous effort of trying to convince the public that women as well as men should have a voice in making the laws which govern them. Unfortunately, the activities of both ladies landed them in jail. The younger suffragette, far from home and friends, sat on the edge of her cot and wept. The old-timer placed her hand on the girl's shoulder. 'Cheer up,' she said, 'You mustn't mind going to jail. That's part of the job. If you feel discouraged, just pray to God. SHE'LL help you.'"

The audience just roared. Even Mr. Watson and Mr. Nichol sitting in the front row laughed. That did the trick; I relaxed so much one would have thought I had given speeches for years.

The next week's *Life* magazine carried a middle page spread of the dais at the luncheon following the meeting. There I sat, the only woman dining with about fifty men. As a result of that picture, I received a flood of fan mail from almost everyone with whom I had ever gone to school, from kindergarten to college; from some of my old Atlanta customers and friends; from soldiers overseas; from strangers proposing marriage; and some from the inevitable cranks who told me to go home where I belonged. Of course, I had no intention of following that suggestion. In fact, part of my message in the speech was that, although I felt the majority of women brought into the workforce during the war would leave once the men returned, I emphasized that I believed women wanted the right to choose whether to continue working or not.

That first speech paved the way for many other addresses over the next ten years. Some aimed to inspire, some told about the ABCs of the workplace, and many included statistics and facts about the economic state of the union, but I always tried to punctuate them with humor. Mr. Nichol gave me some great advice, and I worked hard to perfect my delivery. I tried never to mention IBM in any talk except when addressing IBM personnel.

To gather information for my speeches, I spent many hours in our factories, which made all kinds of equipment for the armed forces. I learned the difference between a punch press, a milling machine, a lathe, and other equipment and got the chance to meet our own "Rosie the Riveter." Many of the women in our plants had never worked in a factory before. I also collected information about the safety devices IBM created for some of the machines. This formed the basis for several talks I gave around the country about safety training for women in factory work.

Invitations to speak came from a variety of places, including schools and business-oriented colleges as well as institutions and organizations involved in the war effort. My popularity by no means reflected any great talent I offered as a speaker, nor was it due to any brilliance of mind (I wished I had both qualities). I simply represented an oddity at the time, a one-of-a-kind phenomenon: the first woman vice president of a large corporation—and a young one, at that. I could speak to young people, as someone they could relate to, hoping to inspire them to achieve their goals. I never forgot, either, that I represented my company before every audience, even though I seldom mentioned the letters IBM. Perhaps this chance to reach young people and inspire them was what Fred Nichol meant by a "golden opportunity."

Me with my older sister, Helen, 1918.

"Local girl makes good," 1943.

First job with IBM in Atlanta, February, 1940.

Here I am, manager of Systems Service, welcoming girls to active service in the field, 1939. Thomas J. Watson Sr. seated at left.

Greeting Bing Crosby, who helped raise funds for war relief, 1942.

Thomas J. Watson, Sr., speaking to a class at Endicott, N.Y., 1943. I am second from left.

Pan American dinner for President Bustamante of Peru, Waldorf Astoria, 1943.

This is a center spread from *Life Magazine's* picture of The National Association of Manufacturers meeting in the Waldorf ballroom, where I spoke in 1943. "2500 Men and Me!" 95

Sitting with Bethlehem Steel executives, 1943.

Thomas J. Watson, Sr., me, and General Knudson, head of General Motors, 1943.

Princess Juliana of the Netherlands, Thomas J. Watson Sr., and me, 1943.

INTERNATIONAL BUSINESS MACHINES CORPORATION
590 MADISON AVENUE
NEW YORK

OFFICE OF
THE PRESIDENT

December 23, 1943

Miss Ruth M. Leach
27 East 79th Street
New York, N. Y.

Dear Miss Leach:

It gives me a great deal of satisfaction to write to you this year as Vice President of the IBM.

I have followed your work very closely since you graduated from the IBM School, and it was soon evident to me that you were a young lady with determination to do a good job. It was this determination and your high ideals and fine character which enabled you to make such rapid progress in our company.

I have always appreciated your constructive suggestions and your loyal cooperation, and in your new position I want you to look upon me as your assistant and to come to me with any problems which you feel I can help you with.

As you know, I am very keenly interested in the women in our organization and want them to have equal opportunity and equal supervision with the men in connection with any work that they are equipped to perform as well as the men. Now that these matters are all in your hands, I am not going to worry about them, because I know they will be handled satisfactorily.

Mrs. Watson joins me in all good wishes to you and your family for the Holiday Season and the coming New Year.

Yours very sincerely,

TJW:HC

Letter from Thomas J. Watson Sr., following my appointment as vice-president, 1943.

Speaking at luncheon following conferring of degrees, Bryant College, 1944. Senator Green seated at right.

Jane Haislip Creel, executive assistant, and me with members of the IBM World Trade Company, 1944.

Howard Chandler Christy (artist), Thomas J. Watson Sr., and me at Grand Central Art Galleries, 1944.

Speaking at Providence IBM office, 1944. Thomas J. Watson Sr., second from the left.

My fourth class, Systems Service Class 555, 1944. Endicott, NY.

National Women's Press Club 10 outstanding women of 1945. Included were Dr. Esther Loring Richards, Agnes de Mille, Dr. Lise Meitner, I.A.R. Wylie, Anne O'Hare McCormick, Margaret Webster, Georgia O'Keeffe, me, Margaret Cuthbert, Dean Virginia Gildersleeve, and Rep. Mary T. Norton.

Speaking at graduation excercises, Endicott, NY, August 1945

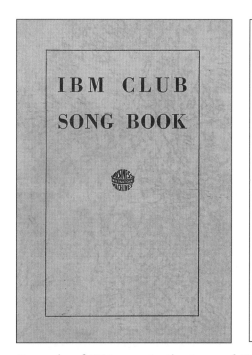

IBM CLUB

SONG BOOK

YOU'RE THE TOP

You're the top, you're a contest winner,
You're the top, you're a Homestead dinner,
You're a Charlie Love, a salesman of renown,
You're a Phillips speech, a Ruthie Leach, you're goin' to town.
You're the top, you're the Do for Douglas,
Like my tent, you're the height of snugness,
You're the leadership the Watsons give to all.
You're the stuff that IBM has on the ball !

You're the top, you're a quota getter !
You're the top, you're a record setter,
You're the Watson Trophy we've tried so hard to get,
If Regueiro got you, Del Rio got you, we'll get you yet.
Points are high, up some more and then some,
Thanks to Jack and his new extension.
You're McPherson's thought, the Red La Motte we hail !
You're an EAM - ITR - ET sale.

You're the top, you're a service bureau,
You're the top, you're a first club hero.
You're the Prospect who put his Ball Point to the line,
You're the demonstration, the application that made him sign.
You're the top, you're a check by Williams,
You're the top, Zolly's points in millions.
You're a member of the biggest club until
Nineteen-fifty ushers in one bigger still.

Example of IBM song to the tune of "You're the Top" by Cole Porter.

Mademoiselle Woman of the Year Awards–I won my award for business. Christmas, 1946. Included were Gwendolyn Brooks and Barbara Bel Geddes. Seated center is the skipper of a ship that won many battles.

Receiving doctor of law degree from Hartwick College, Oneonta, NY, June 9, 1947.

THOMAS J. WATSON

ON HIS COMPLETION OF

A THIRD OF A CENTURY AS

HEAD

OF INTERNATIONAL BUSINESS

MACHINES CORPORATION

August 14, 1947

IBM COUNTRY CLUB · ENDICOTT · NEW YORK

I spoke at this dinner honoring Thomas J. Watson Sr., August 14, 1947.

Seated betweeen General George C. Marshall and Thomas J. Watson Sr., 1948.

Me, Thomas J. Watson Sr.,
and Jarmila Novotna,
Metropolitan Opera star,
1948.

In the board room with Thomas J. Watson Sr. during an executive committee meeting, 1947.

Visiting the new San Jose factory, 1948.

Greeting Dwight Eisenhower at the IBM Hundred Percent sales-men's convention in Endicott, NY, 1948.

RUTH LEACH POLLOCK remembers herself in this 1948 photograph as so nervous that she shook both Dwight Eisenhower's hand and coat sleeve. Thomas J. Watson, founder of IBM is in the center. The occasion was the IBM 100 Percent Club salesmen's convention in Endicott, N.Y. Having Eisenhower at their company celebration was considered quite a coup at that time, since the IBM convention coincided with the National Democratic Convention and in 1948, the Democrats were trying to draft Ike to run on their ticket.

Aids the Met

Vice president of International Business Machines, and treasurer of the Metropolitan Opera Fund for the 1949-50 season.

As vice president of International Business Machines, I was speaker at the Hundred Percent Club, July12, 1949.

STATE OF NEW YORK
EXECUTIVE CHAMBER
ALBANY

THOMAS E. DEWEY
GOVERNOR

June 30, 1951

Miss Ruth Leach
28 East 73rd Street
New York 21, New York

Dear Miss Leach:

It is my honor to reappoint you as a member
of the New York Woman's Council of the New York
State Department of Commerce.

As you know, the Council was formed after the
last war to meet the problem of readjustment to a
peace economy.   Now the new challenge of a defense
emergency brings urgent demands and once more
the assistance of experienced and public spirited
women like you is needed.

It is with great pleasure that I again look
forward to your membership on the distinguished
Council.

With kind personal regards,

Sincerely yours,

Thomas E. Dewey

TED:MD

Letter from Governor Thomas E. Dewey, 1951.

Branch Office Administration Class #1607, September 15, 1952, through
September 19, 1952, Poughkeepsie, NY.

California native daughters honored by Mills College in Oakland, 1952. I received an honorary degree Doctor of Laws. Included are Agnes deMille and Georgia O'Keeffe, center, and Lillian M. Gilbreth, second from left rear row.

Miss Ruth M. Leach
28 East 73rd Street
New York, New York

Dear Miss Leach:

Mrs. Watson joins me in sending to you our greetings for the holiday season and our best wishes for a New Year filled with many blessings.

We know that this will be a particularly happy Christmas for you and we share your joy. Both of us are delighted by the news of your coming marriage. There is no one for whom our wishes for happiness are more sincere, and no one more deserving of the best that life has to offer. We congratulate Mr. Pollack upon choosing one of the finest young women we know, and to both of you we extend our very best wishes for a wonderful life together.

As I write this letter, I wish once again also to express my deep appreciation for the cooperation and assistance which you have always extended to me and to all our associates here at IBM. Your contributions to the Company have been an important factor in our progress, and I congratulate you upon the fine way in which you have always handled your responsibilities. You have reflected credit upon yourself and upon our organization.

At this time of year our hearts are filled with the spirit of this Christmas Season. The perseverance and good will of men everywhere continue to make meaningful the message brought to us by the Prince of Peace, Whose Birth we celebrate. It is the message that serves as a guide for both personal and international relations in the world today, and which, as we approach the new challenges and new opportunities of the coming year, is an inspiration to all right-thinking individuals to renew their efforts in the cause of peace.

Again wishing you and yours every happiness which the Christmas Season brings, and with kindest regards in which Mrs. Watson joins me, I remain.

Sincerely yours,

TJW:reh

Christmas letter from
Thomas J. Watson Sr.,1953

Me, Walter Cronkite, and K Amonette, Golden Circle for
IBM, Vancouver BC, 1994.

Armonk, New York 10504-1783

Louis V. Gerstner, Jr., Chairman and Chief Executive Officer

June 7, 1996

Dear Ruth,

Congratulations on your induction into the Women in Technology
International (WITI) Hall of Fame.

This award highlights the long-term effects of your contributions to
IBM and to the advancement of women in business and industry.

IBM is proud of the recognition for you personally and professionally.

Sincerely,

Lou

Mrs. Ruth Leach Amonette
85...
Ca...

CHAPTER TWELVE

Dancing as Fast as I Can

In February of 1944, another class began in Endicott for seventy systems service women. So I returned to my commuting on the Delaware Lackawanna and again busied myself at my Endicott desk when I wasn't escorting VIPs through the plant. The company continued to provide customer engineering classes and classes for factory workers who wanted instruction on some of the IBM machines manufactured in the factory across the street from the school.

The IBM Washington, DC, office serviced the largest number of big government installations in the country, and Jane Haislip worked there for seven years handling the big customers. As she was Washington's top systems service woman and had great teaching experience, I had hoped to entice her into the teaching program in Endicott, but the factory personnel office grabbed her before I got the chance. She stood out so that the company soon welcomed her to World Headquarters as systems service manager.

Jane and I spent many hours on railroads that spring, visiting offices throughout the country to hire young women for the summer class. But we rarely traveled together. One of us always had to be in Endicott to run the show there. Mary Schultz spent the summer helping to create a pension plan for IBM, but when time permitted, she too helped out with the hiring program.

The IBM sales staff made it a custom to keep in close touch with the field offices. The district managers frequently visited the sales force in each office of their territories. But in wartime, new sales dwindled so there were no district managers. So Mary Schultz, Jane Haislip, or I, along with the Watsons, were about the only contacts with World Headquarters some of the offices had during the late war years. A few special representatives handling utility, oil, or transportation accounts made calls to some offices during this time, but very few. Mr. Watson told me specifically, "Miss Leach, on your visits around the country, try to meet some of IBM's big wartime customers to make sure our offices are handling them properly. They keep IBM going, and I count on your systems service women to see that all of their customers are entirely satisfied with the IBM service that goes along with the rental of our machines. A dissatisfied customer could return a roomful of our equipment at a tremendous loss to the company."

Major wartime installations, such as Wright Air Field in Dayton, Ohio, seemed to require constant assistance in training, programming, and servicing. They couldn't hire enough qualified personnel, so they leaned on us for assistance. We finally put a senior systems service woman in charge and after several weeks, suggested she be put on their payroll instead of ours to solve their problems.

Newark Air Field in New Jersey, another big operation I visited, needed constant help. I couldn't believe how much trouble the people in charge of these big installations had hiring personnel capable of handling the workload. But we managed to supply them temporarily with IBM employees. My job was to direct the systems service women to the installations that needed them most.

A hardworking systems service woman named LaVerne Nunes handled the wartime installations in the Oakland, California area. She covered facilities such as Mare Island Naval Base, the Benicia Arsenal, Basalt Rock Shipyard, and Kaiser Shipyards in Richmond where Liberty ships were built. The payroll departments, particularly at Kaiser, always had trouble getting their weekly pay checks out on time—one hundred thousand of them at Kaiser. LaVerne's assignment meant making sure the companies met those deadlines. A strike or a slowdown would jeopardize vital war production.

I liked to call LaVerne one of IBM's unsung heroines, a woman who worked long hours and weekends, too, to make deadlines and to keep our customers in good shape during wartime. We had many like her, all over the country: Frances Young and Betty Hohf Frank in Chicago; Mary Adelaide Rozelle in New York; Dorothy Lewis in Springfield, Massachusetts; Anne Haislip who handled the entire state of West Virginia, mostly by bus and without a manager; and countless others.

We lived in demanding times, and some stretched their energies to the breaking point, but IBM got its war jobs done in the field offices as well as in the factories. Whenever I had the chance, I commended our personnel for making IBM such an outstanding contributor to the war effort during those difficult days.

The sheer numbers of IBM machines used in installations like those handled by our systems service women were tremendous. Some of the women couldn't handle heavy responsibility and the stress of meeting deadlines for very long. They did better teaching or working on other phases of their job. The IBM salesmen who were not in the military looked after some of the other big accounts and also served as acting managers of IBM field offices.

During one of my tours I visited the Kaiser Shipyards and Henry Kaiser himself showed me the large housing development near the shipyard that he'd built to attract workers from the East and from the southern states. He said, "It's difficult to recruit personnel for shipbuilding from those who proved ineligible for the draft or who have some handicap that prevents them from enlisting. We used up the supply in California, so many of our recruits are mountain folk or farmers, all 4-F, of course."

Some couldn't even read or write; some had never seen a modern bathroom till they moved into the housing development. Mr. Kaiser told me, "One family we had built fires in the bathtub to cook over; they knew no other way to prepare a meal." But, by gum, they got the job done, helping to build all those victory ships that carried our soldiers and equipment overseas to win the war.

Trains, Trains, Trains

Traveling during those years, as I said earlier, could be pretty awful, as anyone who had to use trains in those days will tell you. The government had forbidden air travel to the public unless they had a priority. So, in 1943 I left New York on December 4th and worked my way west to spend Christmas with my family, stopping at various IBM offices along the way. I returned via Portland, Seattle, Minneapolis, Milwaukee, Chicago, and then decided to "do" Texas before returning to New York on February 3rd—all by train.

While in Seattle I visited the Boeing Aircraft plant and learned how many brooms they used in a week to keep the place clean and other statistics I soon forgot. Company representatives escorted visitors along a deck built about twenty-five or thirty feet above the floor along the side of a tremendously long hangar-like building, so that we could watch workers assemble bombers and other military planes from start to finish. As in the shipyards, IBM had an impressive set of accounting machines to handle the huge payroll and other accounting applications for Boeing.

On the leg from Seattle to Minneapolis, which took five days, the trains had all kinds of mechanical problems stemming from frozen pipes. We had a deadly cold winter that year, and from my Pullman window I could see herds of livestock frozen to death out on the range. The train stopped frequently either to take on water or to let workmen thaw out the pipes to get needed water to all bathrooms and particularly to the galley. Unfortunately, I had brought only one book along with me and had finished it by the end of the first day.

"Do you have any books or magazines you're not reading that you'd like to exchange?" I asked the man sitting across from me.

"I'm glad you asked. I've run out of reading material, too. Whoever expected such delays?" And so began an exchange library among the passengers for those five long days and nights.

Most trains I took carried troops transferring from one camp to another or overseas. In Dennison, Texas, my train picked up the largest troop movement I had ever seen—and I saw lots of them. Whenever we stopped, I'd walk up and down the station platform for exercise. At Dennison I counted twenty-four cars on our train, and the troops occupied all but one, which the railroad reserved for civilians. No wonder no trains ever arrived or departed on time. And thank goodness we civilians got our dinner at 5:30 p.m., before the servicemen were fed. The way they ate, we'd have found little food left for us!

On one trip from Los Angeles to Chicago, to my annoyance, I found myself assigned an upper berth, and to make matters worse, when I attempted to climb up to it, someone else had already taken it. Jerry Colona, Paul Lukas, and other men from the Bob Hope Show occupied most of my car. Hope himself traveled on the train ahead of us. While the conductor searched for a berth for me, I amused myself listening to Bob Hope's scriptwriters trying to come up with new ideas for gags. When I finally retired, one of them seemed to be left without a berth, and I suspected I might be sleeping in it, but by then I was past caring.

I complained about my train life to my family in a letter home:

Dear Family—I've been in 13 different hotels during the past month and a half. And if I see another train as long as I live it will be too soon! This should be the last leg of my trip, and I have drawn the following conclusions:

1. *Civilians should not travel during wartime.*
2. *Soldiers and sailors are exceptionally polite and nice on trains.*
3. *Lounge cars should have book-lending libraries on board for people like me—I've read, cover to cover,* Reader's Digest *January and February,* Time, Life, Good Housekeeping, Cosmo-Collins, Vogue, Harpers *and* Redbook.
4. *I still don't like magazine articles.*
5. *Chicago is the dirtiest town. Minneapolis might be all right if it weren't for the 32° below.*
6. *I'd still love to live on a ranch instead of looking at the blueness of sky pinched between two tenement houses.*

7. *Texas is BIG. I like Texas.*
8. *It's imperative to keep one's sense of humor while traveling.*

Filling in for Mr. Watson

During this time, I liked spending my weekends in Manhattan...playing catch-up with my apartment, my friends, laundry, hair appointments, and mail. Saturday mornings I spent at the office (we always worked a half day then) catching up on work there.

About noon one Saturday in April 1944, as I hurried to finish some work so I could go home and get ready for guests I'd invited that evening, Mr. Watson's office called to summon me upstairs. I found him with Mrs. Samuel Rosenman, a member of President Roosevelt's Housing Committee. Her husband wrote all of FDR's speeches. I guessed that Mr. Watson thought it would be a good idea for me to know the lady so I could be appointed to her committee, which raised money to stimulate interest in postwar housing. I was already serving on the popular wartime AWVS (American Women's Volunteer Service) postwar planning committee.

We all three lunched together in his private dining room. Just as we finished, Mr. Watson looked at his watch and said, "Goodness, I promised Mrs. Watson I would meet her and some friends at the Metropolitan Opera House for the afternoon performance. Please, Miss Leach, will you go in my place? I will never make it." Without waiting for an answer he said, "Here's my ticket; you take it." It never occurred to him I might have plans that day, too.

Without returning to clean up my desk, I rushed out the door to a taxi one of his secretaries had waiting on Madison Avenue to take me to the old Met. I found Mrs. Watson in the front of her private box with a couple of children. They all sat listening attentively to "Der Rosenkavalier," which had already begun.

I quickly took my seat, feeling completely out of place, and hoped no one would see me in my Saturday morning work clothes with no hat, no gloves, nor mink coat—*de rigeur* attire for Met boxes in those days. In fact, I looked like Mrs. Watson's cook...not too far from the truth.

I asked Mrs. Watson's delightful sister, Miss Kittredge, sitting beside me in the back row of the box, who was singing.

"Jarmila Novotna," she whispered.

"Who is she?" I asked, and learned she was one of opera's leading sopranos. The children sitting right in front of me were hers. And her husband, Baron Daubek of Prague, Czechoslovakia, sat next to me on my right. What a rare treat for me to meet the Daubek family, despite my embarrassment about my attire, but Mr. Watson should have told me I would be meeting celebrities.

I excused myself early to pick up groceries for the weekend and straighten my apartment before my own guests arrived. Unfortunately, I missed my hair appointment that day.

Running with Mr. Watson

The following Tuesday afternoon, off I went again for Endicott, with the Watson party. Dr. Ben Wood of Columbia University, a frequent speaker to Endicott classes, accompanied us, and he and I spent the entire evening with Mr. Watson in his drawing room on the train discussing a number of subjects. By the time we arrived in Endicott, we had: partitioned Europe, settled the peace program, rehabilitated the world, discussed the race problem, reorganized the U.S. government, elected a new president, and gone through all the interviews Mr. Watson had had with Mussolini, Hitler, and just about every royal person in the world. Mr. Watson confessed, "You know, at some of those European affairs before the war, I would just plain run out of 'queen language.'"

We spent a typically strenuous week in Endicott. Mr. Watson, a human dynamo, went on and on through the day and night, talking all the time, on less sleep than anyone I ever knew. He made an average of two speeches a day, spent hours in the factory, gave a luncheon each day, ate with the girls in the class and talked to them each night at the Homestead into the wee hours. Then after that, he wanted to report to me about his impressions of the class.

Charlie Kirk, vice president in charge of manufacturing, accompanied Mr. Watson most of the time when he was in the factory. But when he visited my side of the street, I always accompanied him around the school. I could set up a large room for speaking programs pretty fast by now, with the practice I'd had. When the boss came to speak and the students all assembled, I would ask someone else to lead the IBM songs. Mr. Watson loved those songs, thought they built company spirit. I didn't make a good cheerleader though, plus I couldn't carry a tune. Besides, I considered all the singing and rah-rah rather juvenile.

(From 1940 IBM song booklet)

There's a thrill in store for all,
For we're about to toast
The corporation that we represent.
We're here to cheer each pioneer
And also proudly boast
Of that "man of men," our sterling president.
The name of T.J. Watson means a courage none can stem:
And we feel honored to be here to toast the "I.B.M."

Chorus
EVER ONWARD–EVER ONWARD!
That's the spirit that has brought us fame!
We're big, but bigger we will be,
We can't fail for all can see
That to serve humanity has been our aim!
Our products now are known in every zone,
Our reputation sparkles like a gem!
We've fought our way through—and new
Fields we're sure to conquer too
For the EVER ONWARD I.B.M.

At the end of that week, I returned to New York exhausted and, as usual, a mess—circles under my eyes, hair desperately in need of a shampoo, party dress dirty, and no hot water in my apartment because of a broken pipe.

Naturally, Mrs. Watson chose that evening to ask me to help entertain Victor Boacas, head of IBM Brazil, at a formal dinner party at the River Club. Thank heavens the Watsons offered to pick me up, as a freak snowstorm had blown in. Taxis were always at a premium around dinnertime, and I hated riding the bus around town in my long evening dress.

* * *

Life in the corporate world of IBM was strenuous for a lone woman living in two places, New York and Endicott. I had busy desks in both locations, and I also traveled all over the country visiting IBM offices, interviewing, and sometimes giving speeches, not to mention accommodating a demanding boss. Spending any length of time with Mr. Watson always wore me down. IBM corporate culture really centered on our leader's decisions on every phase of the business, and on which of us would be instructed to direct those decisions to their completion.

Dear Family—I spent almost all of Tuesday in T.J.'s office in conference about everything. I swear that man can think of more things to do—and because I happen to be there, he tells me to do all the things.

It seemed as if IBM was my life twenty-four hours a day, with no escape. I grew so tired of trains and buses and having to break dates with friends because the daily IBM hustle left me no time for a private life. A long break sounded heavenly.

CHAPTER THIRTEEN

A Vacation at Last

By the middle of May 1944, I needed a vacation. My friend Augusta, asked if I knew of anyone in IBM who might want to help her drive Montgomery Clift's Buick out to Hollywood, where he was working. Augusta's husband, Kevin, was there too making a movie of the U.S. Army Air Force stage hit "Winged Victory." How I longed to get away and do something different for a change of pace. So I said, "Augusta, I know just the person—me! I'd love to join you, and I really need something like this. I'll ask Mr. Watson for permission to go and let you know tomorrow."

My boss got so intrigued with our trip that he started planning it for us. "I think it would be nice for you to stop en route at some of our small IBM offices as well as the one in St. Louis. They haven't had a visit from Headquarters in a long time, so why don't I call and arrange for a lunch or dinner there."

I could see his mind going a mile a minute, filling in every detail of our journey. I had to break in and stop him.

"Mr. Watson, first let me explain that this is my friend's trip, and I am just going along to help her drive. She's arranged to meet another friend of ours along the way in New Mexico, who'll join us for the rest of the trip to Hollywood. I don't think we have the time or gas to take any side trips." I didn't tell him this was one trip I really didn't want to visit any IBM offices.

Then I went on, "Secondly, Mr. Watson, the rationing board would take a dim view of your idea," and I explained the workings of the rationing board. "They distribute gas coupons in a strict fashion; not everyone can get them. If Augusta is moving from New York to Los Angeles, as she is temporarily, the board looks at a map for the shortest distance between the two points. In this case it's Highway 66. Then they determine how many miles we'll be traveling and how much gasoline we'll need to get there. So with the gas coupons allotted to her, we really cannot deviate from Highway 66."

Mr. Watson never drove; he always used trains. So my long explanation of this exotic topic seemed to satisfy him. He wished me well and told me to be careful and drive the "Victory" speed limit of thirty-five miles per hour.

The wartime travel restrictions required everyone to explain the nature of any proposed trip: it had to be a necessity, such as moving a residence, going to a close relative's funeral, illness in the family, and other dire situations. On Highway 66, we passed a lot of hearses. Crooks used the big ominous vehicles to transport certain forbidden merchandise, like liquor, from one state to another.

On the Road

Augusta and I had a wonderful time on that trip, our first driving tour across the country. We tried to distinguish igneous, sedimentary, and metamorphic rock, and spot alluvial fans, stratification of rock, and other tidbits we'd learned in Geology 1A. We also tried to identify trees and recall what little we knew of flowering plants along the way. The architectural changes we saw as the countryside changed amazed us. And we loved studying people as we drove through the various towns.

The car radio failed to work at all the first day out, so when we stopped for gas, we joined others gathered around the station's radio listening to the war news. In Terre Haute, Indiana, when we arose at 4:45 a.m. on June 6th, we heard the landing of the troops in Normandy on the radio in our hotel room. The sound of D-Day gunfire echoed in the background, as if we sat on a landing craft with the troops. Whenever we got the chance along the way, we listened to news of the war, and eagerly followed our army's penetration into France, pushing the Germans back. I remember hearing about the bloody and horrifying Battle of the Bulge, the Germans' last stand in World War II.

One of our tires blew out on the highway not far from Tulsa. Traffic was sparse, so we decided to change it ourselves rather than risk flagging down a stranger for help. As we began removing our luggage from the trunk to get to the spare tire, I said to Augusta, "Who are we kidding? I don't know a wrench from a lug bolt. Don't you think we look kind of cute and helpless? Someone's bound to stop, and I say, let 'em help!" And of course, someone did.

Our Good Samaritan put on the spare, but the tire that blew was beyond repair. We hesitated to face a long trip through the desert without a spare, but replacement of a tire during the war required the permission of the rationing board of the area.

"I said I didn't want to see an IBM office on this trip, but I can change my mind. Let's find the Tulsa office; I'm sure they can help."

Clad in shorts and sneakers, with my hair in pigtails, I approached a rather startled IBM manager. "Sir," I said, "you don't recognize me in my traveling attire, but my picture is on your wall. I'm Ruth Leach." I pointed to a photograph of myself with other IBM executives. He peered at the picture and then at me. I continued, "I'm driving with a friend to California, and we're in trouble. We desperately need a new tire. Can you help us out?"

Lucky for us he knew the mayor of Tulsa well, so he took Augusta to meet him. The mayor introduced her to the Tulsa rationing board, and she used her dramatic ability to win them over. They all lunched together while I stayed behind and had a hamburger with the young ladies in the IBM office. We lost three and a half hours in driving time, but we got our new tire.

Augusta said one day as we neared the Texas panhandle, "Remind me when we get to the border to call the number my friend gave me in New York. We might be able to pick up some extra gas coupons."

"If we don't get any," I warned, "it means we can't leave this highway and pick up Jeanne." But Augusta's phone call proved successful. We got the coupons and turned off Route 66 toward Hobbs, New Mexico, to pick up our friend Jeanne Green, who was dying to join us and grab a little holiday from her husband's miserably hot air base in the southern part of the state.

Neither Augusta nor I had ever been to Hobbs before, and the only place Jeanne could think of to meet us was in front of the local prophylactic station. Every town next to an army camp or air base had one where soldiers could go to get protection against the spread of sexually transmitted diseases.

I had the wheel at the time and as we approached a waiting crowd at a stop signal in Hobbs, I said to Augusta, "When I slow down, lower your window and ask where their prophylactic station is." You should have seen the looks we got. It took three stops before anyone would pay any attention to us. But we found Jeanne just where she said she'd be and continued on our way. Our friends and family got a lot of laughs over the "Hobbs incident."

We found no motels to speak of in the East or Midwest, and anything resembling a motel was usually occupied for the duration by families of soldiers stationed nearby. So, we always stopped driving each day around 4 p.m. to find a room for the night, which wasn't easy. We established a routine of first getting a room, then taking a walk and any other exercise we could find, showering and changing for dinner.

We retired early so we could get up and be on the road by 5 or 5:30 the next morning. Since nothing was open at that hour for breakfast, we ate what was left over from dinner the night before, usually rolls and fruit.

Traveling by private car certainly beat those dirty trains and buses I had been using. With one eye on the rear view mirror, Augusta and I managed occasionally to exceed the 35 mph speed limit. We even sneaked in a peak at the Grand Canyon as we drove through Arizona, coasting when we could to save gasoline. We made Los Angeles in seven and a half days, much to the relief of Kevin, and Monty Clift, who was happy to see his car in the same condition he'd left it.

Dear Family—We sure had fun driving across. I must say quite relaxing, because we changed off every two or three hours and each of us took naps at least twice during the day. No warm weather nor rain did we have at all. I've been in one spot now for four days and I still wake up each morning thinking I must be off to make our 400 miles for the day!

We found Kevin on the set of "Winged Victory" and spent the rest of the day watching the cast rehearse. I had fun catching up with some of the old group I had met in New York when I first arrived in 1941. For three days Augusta, Jeanne and I fixed barbecue dinners in Kevin's rented house for our friends in the cast to give them some home cooking for a change. Then, after a short visit in the San Francisco Bay Area with my parents, my sister and her family, I returned by train to New York, all refreshed from my wild but fun vacation.

* * *

The happy glow of my vacation quickly faded as I opened the door to my apartment and found I'd been robbed. From the looks of the dresser and closet in total disarray, the thief must have wanted money. When he found none, he decided to take my beaver coat instead, and other things he could pawn. I lost a few trinkets of jewelry, mostly of sentimental value. But more importantly, I lost my peace of mind. I now wanted better security, a place with a doorman for protection, particularly for evenings when I returned late from Waldorf dinners.

After another frustrating search, I finally found an unfurnished apartment at 28 East 73rd Street at Madison Avenue (my third move in a little over a year). I bought furniture from my friend, Jeanne Herman, when she returned to San Francisco for the duration of the war while her husband was at sea. So I was once again ensconced in a cozy, attractive, ideally located duplex apartment, with doormen for security. I could walk easily to and from work, and on weekends, if I wanted, I could stroll through Central Park a block away. Believe it or not, we felt perfectly safe in the park then, even women alone at night. Times certainly changed.

CHAPTER FOURTEEN

The Long Hot Summer Of '44

On June 13, 1944, the Rochester Athenaeum and Mechanical Institute(MI), now called the Rochester Institute of Technology, invited me to set a new precedent by delivering the commencement address. I felt thrilled to be the first woman ever to give the principal address at an MI convocation. What's more, I gave it from the pulpit in the First Presbyterian Church in Rochester, New York, a big first for me.

It really flattered me when the Institute's president wanted to give me a check for $500 for making a speech. "Oh, no, President Ellinger, I couldn't accept. IBM doesn't allow any of its employees to take remuneration for making speeches."

Then he asked, "Would you accept, then, a painting of your selection from our art gallery of student paintings?" Delighted, I chose a beautiful snow scene and enjoyed it for many years.

In July, we kicked off another successful systems service class in Endicott, with Loraine McLennan in charge this time. In my last coast-to-coast trip, I had covered a lot of territory and found some good applicants for the school.

On opening day, I gave my usual talk to the group about how we conduct ourselves while living at the Homestead under the same roof with IBM customers, mostly men attending special one- or two-week classes.

"Always treat these men courteously even though they may not be to your liking: they represent our bread and butter. And if they invite you to go downtown somewhere," I cautioned "please refuse in your most gracious way. This is really no place to start any kind of a relationship between a man away from his family and a much younger lady on her way to becoming an IBM systems service woman. To do so could threaten your reputation as well as IBM's.

"Many doors have opened to women during this war because of the shortage of men. You have been chosen to help fill those vacancies in the field offices to the best of your ability, and to protect IBM's business.

"When you complete your studies here, you will leave equipped to handle that responsibility with knowledge and tact. In fact, for the first time in your life, you may face reality in the workplace, and your arena will be a man's world." One of the young women must not have been listening to me that day about not going out with an IBM customer while in Endicott. When Mr. Watson drove up to the Homestead the next evening around 9:30 p.m., who should he see walking along the drive from the highway but one of our students and a customer she had obviously met at the Homestead.

He called me immediately and told me to reprimand the girl harshly but not to fire her. I made a bed check that night and found this same student unaccounted for, so I called her into my office the next morning. I explained once more why we had certain rules, and told her Mr. Watson had spotted her the night before when he drove up the drive.

"When I spoke to the whole class about IBM's rules of etiquette while living at the Homestead, did you not hear me tell your class we didn't want any of you going out with customers?"

After a long pause, she answered, "Well, Miss Leach, you know how it was when you were young." I knew immediately that anyone with as little tact as she had would get nowhere in this business. Besides, I was only two years older than she. Needless to say, she didn't last long in the company.

On the War Front

With Mussolini dead, and German officers attempting to assassinate Hitler, it had become obvious Der Führer had begun losing more than ground, especially after he lost Italy to our side. News trickled over the German lines about the horrors of the holocaust and the millions of Jews who had been killed. The stories we heard made us all want to work harder to defeat this maniac who had caused so much grief in the world. We knew he couldn't possibly hold out much longer.

We heard equally grim news from the Pacific in 1944, but unlike in Europe, our efforts against Japan seemed to be meeting with less success. Fighting this jungle and naval war left our many battleships in Pacific waters prey to Japanese kamikaze pilots and torpedoes from Japanese submarines.

IBM supplied machines everywhere in both the European and Pacific theaters. Mobile machine records units carried IBM punched card accounting machines mounted in large vans with their own generators to power the machines. These units kept track of Army and Navy personnel and performed other accounting applications. It became difficult at times to camouflage the large vans and prevent enemy aircraft from spotting them. But in spite of the German government's orders to capture one of our mobile units intact so they could gain access to our personnel records, not one got blown up or captured during the entire war.

Taking the Heat

Bryant College in Providence, Rhode Island, invited Mr. and Mrs. Watson, Mary, and me to its 81st annual commencement exercises to be held on Friday, August 4, 1944. Senator Alben Barkley of Kentucky, the Senate majority leader (and later vice president of the U.S.), gave the commencement speech to the 155 graduates, mostly women. Senator Barkley and I received honorary degrees that day, along with Miss Anna Griffith, administrator of child welfare in Rhode Island. The day was without a doubt the hottest in the history of Providence, and we had to wear woolen caps and gowns over our clothing. The klieg lights above us didn't help, either, in that non-air-conditioned hall.

Senator Theodore Francis Green of Rhode Island introduced his colleague, Senator Barkley, to the audience. Howard McGrath, the governor of Rhode Island, also sat on the dais, along with IBM's Mr. Watson.

Dear Family—Sat next to Senator Barkley today. He's a howl! Has a swell sense of humor. He forgot for a moment he was at a commencement and talked for over an hour. When I bade him farewell later that day, he insisted I call on him when I come to Washington, D.C. Can't you see me calling on the Majority Leader of the U.S. Senate?!

At the luncheon in honor of the degree recipients following the convocation, I went looking for my place card, only to find they had seated all four ladies at the head table together way down at the end. After talking for some time with our host, Dr. Jacobs before we sat down, I suggested, "Why don't we mix the ladies in with the men so they don't look so conspicuous down there alone at the end of the table?" I really wanted to sit by at least a senator or a governor. So Dr. Jacobs changed the seating, and I sat between him and Senator Green, and Mrs. Watson sat between the governor and Senator Barkley, as it should have been. Dr. Jacobs thanked me and said the head table looked better that way.

During lunch I gave our host some more gentle advice. "You know, Dr. Jacobs, you made a big mistake today by not giving an honorary degree to Mr. Watson instead of to me."

Dr. Jacobs looked startled. "Really? Why do you say that?"

"You probably would have received a much larger monetary gift from IBM than you will from me. My advice to you is to invite him next year as a recipient of an honorary degree. Then see what happens." He did just that, and proved me right.

Following lunch a representative escorted us in the governor's limousine to Camp Endicott, the Navy training center, Camp Thomas, and the Quonset Naval Air Base twenty miles away. We put on a good show, as we sped through the countryside there, complete with naval escorts, jeeps, motorcycles, flags and sirens. I felt like Commando Kelly returning from Italy a hero, except the crowds weren't yelling. They stood wondering who the heck we were.

Mrs. Watson felt wilted by heat, as did I. She asked me, "Why don't you suggest we go up in the control tower, even if just the two of us go. I hear it's air conditioned up there, and we could cool off."

"A great idea, Mrs. Watson. I'll see that we get there, and you think up some questions to ask so we can stay up there longer."

After cooling off in the tower, Mrs. Watson and I joined the group at the Walsh Kaiser Yard to see the launching of the U.S.S. Circe, a large combat cargo vessel, then on to the home of the captain of the naval base for soft drinks. By the time we arrived at the Providence IBM office clam bake at 7 p.m., with no time to change our wet clothes and clean up, we felt pretty well exhausted by the heat and all the festivities of that very long day. But Mr. Watson looked as fresh as ever in his starched white collar, wool suit, and vest. He never seemed to mind the heat and rarely seemed to tire.

The IBM offices, usually so delighted to see the Watsons on their visits around the country, always gave a luncheon or dinner in their honor. And what could be more typical of this region of the U.S. than a clam bake...and the Providence office went all out, starting with clam bouillon, clam chowder, steamed clams, filet of sole, lobster and ending up with Indian pudding. What a feast! But I felt too tired, dripping hot and sticky to enjoy all that food. The IBM office presented me with a lovely gift, a matching pin and earrings set, but I kept my thanks brief because I knew Mr. Watson would speak and that could well go on for another hour.

Back in New York, the city had begun to cool down, and life resumed its normal pace, with more spirited meetings in Mr. Watson's office. We had many heated arguments, and I saw some men crucified under our leader's attacks. I used to cringe when tempers rose and wondered why such confrontations could not have been peacefully resolved in some other way.

In the fall of '44, Mr. Watson called me to his office and asked,

"Miss Leach, have you thought about any post-war planning for your department? How many women do you think will leave IBM when the war ends? How many do you think will want to continue in sales?" I had to confess I hadn't analyzed our personnel that way, but I certainly would do it. Mr. Watson said, "Why don't you write up something of an analysis of the personnel: how many will leave when the war ends, who are promotional material, sales material, etc."

Not long after our discussion, Mr. Watson, who had been in bed with a bad cold, called a meeting at his home of all the special representatives, heads of departments, and executives, including me, the lone woman. He asked me to bring my folder on post-war planning. When I arrived at the meeting, I noticed no one else had a folder, and I began to suspect something.

A discussion of post-war planning ensued, during the course of which our leader asked, "Have any of you gentlemen thought about if the war ended tomorrow, how that would affect your department?" No one stirred. No one said a word. "I just cannot understand why no one here this morning has even thought about the future of this business when the war ends." As he went on he raised his voice and became enraged. Finally, he looked in my direction and said, "Miss Leach, what do you have in your lap?"

I practically whispered, "An analysis of the systems service personnel, sir."

"Well, will you please read it aloud?" I knew I was destined to play a part in this scene, and so I reluctantly took my cue.

I felt so upset at being used to make a point, I could hardly read the darn report. When I finished, he said, "Miss Leach has put all of you to shame!" He ranted on and shamelessly chastised those men, but I couldn't absorb what he said.

My first reaction: What will all my friends here think? As the new kid on the block, I looked up to these senior executives, such as Jack Kenney, Barney Freeman, Gordon Roberts, Al Williams and others, as my mentors. I relied on their judgment when I needed help. Did they now think I was playing teacher's pet in a scheme to embarrass them?

When the meeting ended, I apologized to some of those present, but they seemed not the least bit angry with me. They had seen Mr. Watson use this method of driving a point home before. Jack Kenney said, "Ruth, please don't worry about it. We've been through this kind of thing more than once. We understand he set you up, really." But I felt nearly devastated. I never could tolerate this explosive confrontational style of management. I considered it destructive and believed the same results could be gained from a more sober, supportive and common-sense approach.

At other times, however, I saw employees promoted to heights to which they had never dared aspire. Mr. Watson always put a lot of faith in human relationships, and he rewarded many of us very well.

CHAPTER FIFTEEN

1945—A Year to End All Years

The inexorable march of events in 1945 changed a lot of plans around the world. In February, President Roosevelt, Winston Churchill and Joseph Stalin all met at the famous Yalta Conference in Crimea and agreed that Russia would enter the war against Japan. A week later U.S. Marines landed on Iwo Jima, and a month later U.S. forces invaded Okinawa.

In April, while in Warm Springs, Georgia, President Roosevelt suffered a cerebral hemorrhage and died. Harry S. Truman became President of the United States.

The Russians and Americans took Berlin and won the Battle of the Bulge, and on May 7th Germany surrendered, making May 8th V-E (Victory in Europe) Day. The world could finally celebrate the end of World War II in Europe.

The following morning, Mr. Watson called three of us to his office and said, "What joy today brings to the world, knowing the fighting in Europe has ended. Now, I want to send felicitations to all my friends there, particularly those important figures involved in this momentous occasion. So, I am asking for your help to compose some cablegrams for me, and here is my list: Winston Churchill, prime minister of England, Anthony Eden, foreign secretary of England, His Royal Highness King George VI of England, King Leopold of Belgium, King Peter of Romania, King Gustav of Sweden, Queen Wilhelmina and Princess Juliana of the

Netherlands, and Charlotte of Luxembourg. I also want telegrams sent to President Truman and the Honorable Edward Stettinius, our secretary of state.

"Now, divide these names up among you three and return the cablegrams here with the proper addresses and salutations as soon as you can. I want to get them off this morning. Thank you all."

I wondered why he didn't put one of his secretaries to work on this secretarial job, but they all seemed busy sending heaps of messages to other friends for Mr. Watson.

You can well imagine the letter I wrote home that night about how their baby spent the day sending cables to all the kings and queens and prime ministers of Europe, and that my "king and queen" language was pretty rusty.

Shortly after V-E Day in May, Robert Lund, head of the National Association of Manufacturers when I spoke at their convention the previous December, invited me to attend an 8 a.m. breakfast meeting at the Waldorf-Astoria for Junior Achievement. This was an organization for high school students eager to learn the specifics of running a business on their own. Member companies and corporations encouraged and counseled them.

The group called the meeting hoping to spark those present to sponsor Junior Achievement "companies" within their own organizations. The attendees included many high powered CEOs of the time: Elizabeth Arden (Mrs. Graham), Bayard Colgate of Colgate-Palmolive; James A. Farley, of Democratic party fame; Roy Moore, president of Canada Dry; Alfred Fuller, president of Fuller Brush Co.; Craig Sheaffer of Sheaffer Pen Co.; and others. I suspected I was there in place of Mr. Watson.

When Mr. Lund later persuaded Mr. Watson to give a luncheon to introduce his business friends to this worthy cause, Mr. Watson asked me to take responsibility for the whole event, to be given in mid-June at the Metropolitan Club in New York. This brought back memories of my assignments in Endicott planning those large dinners for our graduating classes, only the guests this time were top U. S. business leaders. I spent the next few weeks gathering statistics and information for Mr. Watson's speech; making suggestions about whom to invite; sorting out who should take precedence; deciding whether or not to serve wine and cock-tails; planning the menu; hiring photographers and stenotypists; arranging for recordings of the entire proceedings; and a thousand and one other things. Thank heavens for my dear secretary, Lillian Schumm.

The seating arrangement proved quite a challenge. I said to Mr. Watson, "We have so many corporate heads coming to your luncheon, I don't know whether it would be more diplomatic to seat these men together by industry or by their status in *Forbes* magazine. What do you think I should do?" He looked over the acceptances and told me who was to sit at the head table and left the rest to me.

My list of last minute phone calls of acceptances and regrets had only a tenuous correlation to who actually showed up. No wonder we had some near-mishaps.

The name of the very first guest to arrive didn't appear on any of my lists. Mr. Watson introduced me to a Mr. Ralph Gallagher, president of Standard Oil of New Jersey. "Miss Leach, will you escort this gentleman to his place?" And of course he had none. I sneaked away for a moment, wrote a place card for him and put it at my place in the back of the room.

Next came Henry Kaiser of California who had definitely regretted. "Miss Leach," Mr. Watson said, "here is your old California friend. Would you escort him to his place at the HEAD table?" I seated Mr. Kaiser in IBM Executive V.P. Charlie Kirk's place next to Beardsly Ruml of Macy's, the author of the "Pay-as-you-go Tax Plan." When Charlie appeared I told him he had to sit elsewhere in a "no-show" place or with me out in the hall.

We had a good meeting in spite of the mishaps, and Mr. Watson let the product speak for itself, namely, the high school students, who told of their experiences running their own companies. The self-confidence and verve of those young people really impressed the audience, which included New York's outstanding businessmen. They would not forget what Junior Achievement stood for after that presentation. These young students impressed, too, with their level of interest and commitment.

After the luncheon, I returned to my office for meetings with the head of IBM Brazil and the head of IBM's Real Estate department, meetings that lasted well into the dinner hour. . .business as usual in those days.

Celebrating an End to War

On August 6, the U.S. dropped the atomic bomb on Hiroshima, and a few days later dropped another on Nagasaki. Finally, on August 15th, the Japanese surrendered. The city of Manhattan then proceeded to joyously, almost deliriously, celebrate V-J Day. People filled the streets celebrating the end of World War II. I wrote to my family about the madness:

> *Dear Family—What a day! And what a mess all of Manhattan is, too! I have never seen such a delightful case of mob hysteria before, and probably never will again. Friends invited me to a dinner party up on East 89th Street, and Third Avenue was in an uproar—pure chaos. Flags flew everywhere, and free drinks flowed out of every bistro, with drunken masses of humanity all over the street.*

> *About 10 p.m. we decided to drive downtown to see what was going on. The Park Avenue area around the Waldorf was a madhouse, so we hesitated to venture over to Times Square. We ended the evening with friends at Beekman Tower over by the East River and 49th Street. From their terrace high up we could still hear the roar of the crowds below. Manhattan that very clear evening was a lovely sight—all its buildings aglow with lights, just as the movies always portray the city.*

Back at my apartment that night, I received a phone call from two old friends who had just arrived in town and were frightened at the madness of New York on V-J night. Marian Sproul and Miriam Kropp, on loan from IBM's systems service department to the State Department, had been serving in Lima, Peru, during the war as economic analysts, and were en route home. Having taken a transport from Rio de Janeiro to Norfolk, VA, they had just arrived in New York in time for the celebration.

The two spent about ten days with me getting reoriented to life in the U.S. As Marian said, "You can't imagine what a difference three years makes in hair styles, clothing, food rationing, music, and life in general. It all seems so new to us." Our returning G.I.s had similar reactions after two or three years overseas. They found home much changed.

A few days after arriving in New York, Marian had an emotional family reunion in my apartment. Her father, Robert Gordon Sproul, who had been president of the University of California at Berkeley when we were students there, was returning from representing President Truman at the Reparations Committee meeting in Moscow. Marian's brother, whom she had not seen in four years, came down from Boston to join his sister and father for a gala get-together. Miriam and Marian also spent a day with Mr. and Mrs. Watson at their summer home in Connecticut, and even visited in Endicott before returning to their homes in California.

Throughout their stay, they captivated me with their descriptions of life in Lima, its slow pace, its customs, the war years without rationing. We all talked about our delight that the war was finally over. Helping to reintegrate my friends into normal life in America made me ask myself, "What was normal?" I found I almost didn't know myself, as I certainly hadn't led a normal life during the war years.

War Stories

After the war, the classes in Endicott began to look different than those conducted throughout most of the war. Some IBM people from the Pacific Rim countries who had survived the harsh treatment of Japanese internment camps came to Endicott to be retrained, so they could return to their normal lives. Servicemen from Europe began drifting back as well.

Mr. and Mrs. Eddie Yarborough, our representatives in Manila, had been first interned in the Santo Tomas Camp and later transferred to the Los Banos Camp. They visited Endicott shortly after V-J Day, and shared their diary of experiences in the Philippines under Japanese occupation with the students in a morning meeting of all classes. When the Japanese decamped on January 8, 1945, they left the interned Americans with no way to get home. The internees renamed their compound "Camp Freedom" and established their own laws and chose their own leaders. Their struggle for food and for the physical strength to exist until American troops arrived made our wartime privations seem only a slight inconvenience.

Also in Endicott was Dr. Carlson, president of Silliman University, located during the war about four hundred miles south of Manila. When we met I asked him, "And in which camp were you interned, Dr. Carlson?" He briefly told me how his life had been different from those held in internment camps. "My family and I were part of a group of 14 Americans and Europeans who, rather than let the Japanese capture and torture us, joined the Filipino guerrillas up in the hills. For two years we survived by living in caves and primitive camps like Stone Age tribes. Eventually, we managed to escape the islands by submarine, even before General MacArthur's return."

When I heard this synopsis of his wartime life in the Philippines, I introduced him to the students so they could hear how he had endured the war years.

Late in July, a group of twenty-five men arrived for a sales class in the typewriter division. Many were returning veterans, predominantly from the Air Corps. One of these men had been in the 15th Air Corps in Italy, where he knew an Icelandic girl, Kristin Bjornsdottir, who got caught in the war in Italy while visiting a friend. She had escaped from her German prison camp in Italy and fled to the hills overlooking Salerno, where she hid in a cave until the Americans took the hill from the Germans. Until they could figure out how to get her home via the U.S., the 15th Air Corps used her as an interpreter, since she spoke English, German, Italian, and other languages.

In a strange series of events, through my roommate's friends in the Air Force, Kristin, arriving in New York by Army transport, landed in my living room. For several nights she slept on my sofa and I had another reorientation case on my hands. I found her an attractive, intelligent young lady. So I decided to hire her and send her to the systems service school, so later she could work for us in Iceland. When that Air Force veteran who first told us about her showed up in Endicott that same summer, he sure was surprised to find Kristin there, too.

When I returned from Endicott to New York City to attend some postwar planning meetings, I learned that *Mademoiselle* magazine planned to give me its "Woman of the Year" award in the field of business. Business? I thought. These days all my work seems to be "in the field of reorientation."

Soon after that, I returned by train to Endicott for a gala graduation ceremony. Mary Schultz, Charlie Kirk, and I sat in Charlie's drawing room all the way up, discussing the upcoming festivities and future classes. The Watsons, plus the entire board of directors, Madame Jarmila Novotna, the opera singer, and her husband, Baron Daubek, arrived en masse on Friday night. By doing a nose count, I could see that Saturday would be a long day of speeches, running well into the night, and it was. I finally hit the bed about 2:30 a.m.

Staying over Sunday to get some rest, I took the dreaded sleeper down to New York to be on hand for the big luncheon at the Waldorf-Astoria ballroom on Monday in honor of General Charles de Gaulle. IBM had two tables, but about 85 percent of the 1500 people attending were French. Wild with excitement, they stood on the tabletops and knocked over glassware as they shouted, "Vive la France!"

In all my Waldorf days, I'd never experienced such a scene before. Then when the General appeared on stage to take his seat, all the French in the audience shouted again, this time, "Vive General de Gaulle!" To amuse our table, Charlie Kirk, whose English wasn't always the most proper, kept muttering, "Braaavo, Charlie," with a broad "A" cutting through the French "vives."

The menu looked so elegant in French (*le poulet aux champignons avec petit pois*) that I could hardly wait for lunch to be served. Alas, it was the same old Waldorf chicken and peas we

IBMers had been eating for years.

Mayor LaGuardia, affectionately known then as the "Little Flower," spoke. Then he introduced the General, and the crowd went wild again for several minutes. De Gaulle spoke *en français* to thank us (and the entire U.S.A.) for what we did for France during World War II. At the reception afterwards, the F.B.I. men circulated through the crowd admonishing us, "Kindly do not shake the General's hand, kindly do not shake the General's hand...." My approach, when I reached the head of the receiving line was merely to say, "Bonjour, General." To which he replied with a smile, "Bonjour," towering a foot or two over us all. It was a big day in Manhattan, and the city went all out for the General.

One day in October of 1945, on my way to LaGuardia Airport in the IBM limousine with Vice President Roy Stephens and his wife, we noticed traffic had come to a standstill on Riverside Drive. As we soon learned, President Truman was reviewing the fleet from his cruiser, and the Hudson River overflowed with warships. As the president passed each ship, it saluted with 21 guns. Never had I heard such noise nor seen such mobs of humanity, all struggling to get a better view of our commander-in-chief. Scenes like this made New York City such an exciting place to live. You never knew what you'd see next.

We finally made it to the airport to welcome IBMers Jack Kenney and Peggy Bulmer back from Europe, arriving on an Army transport.

Jack was the first U.S. civilian businessman allowed into Germany after the war, and Peggy, who was in the first systems service class and a linguist, went along as Jack's interpreter.

Jack, a real guiding spirit to us women during the war years, generously shared his IBM experience and knowledge of the business. A top salesman and able executive, he had the courage of his convictions, and handled every assignment Mr. Watson gave him with fairness and dignity. His associates all held him in high esteem. IBM sent Jack to Europe to appraise what was left of our foreign business and to suggest what priorities the company should follow when we began to rebuild.

What tales Jack and Peggy had to tell of the devastation and the horrors of war. They had traveled from Norway and Sweden to France, Switzerland, Italy, Madrid, and London. (Altogether, I had traveled about the same distance going back and forth between New York City and Endicott during the war years, and that didn't include my travels around the country.)

A few nights after Jack and Peggy's arrival, the U.S. Strategic Bombing Survey group arrived at my home. Stan Crandall, husband of our prize instructor in Endicott and a good friend of mine, called and said, "Hi, Ruth. We've just arrived from Europe and wondered if we could come by and say hello over a cocktail."

Of course I was delighted by the visit; I just needed a half hour or so to change my clothes as I'd just gotten home myself. Changed and washed, I looked in the kitchen to see what I could offer as a welcome-back-to-America libation. There were four of us, and all I could find was an inch of gin, a little bit of sherry, two cokes, and one bottle of beer. But it was too late to run to the store.

Stan's friends were Col. Tom Sunderland, in charge of the survey, and a Col. Stevenson, the son-in-law of General Knudsen, whom I had met earlier in Endicott. The three were attached to the Strategic Bombing Survey, a project performed completely on IBM machines. We had a silly time polishing off my meager stores, after which they kindly invited me to the Wedgewood Room of the Waldorf for dinner and dancing. I had a great time with three handsome men all to myself, and never felt so popular, though I was home in bed by 10:30. I could have stayed up all night listening to their tales, but they had been flying a good fifteen hours or more in an army transport and were exhausted.

For three years, my roommates and I had been sending our friends off to battle overseas. Now the pendulum had begun swinging the other way. We eagerly welcomed them home from the war, but we wondered how many were never coming back. Peter McCormack, my "knight on the white horse," had fought his last battle in Italy and lost, as did a few others we all knew well. Though Peter and I weren't officially engaged, we had discussed marriage. I cried for two weeks when I learned of his death. He had a wonderful family in Canada, who had taken me in with open arms and loving hearts. This poor family had suffered tremendously thanks to the war. Peter's sister, Frances, was engaged to a young man the Germans held as a prisoner of war for three years.

I visited with Peter's family a few months after a sniper's bullet ended his life as he took the place of a fellow soldier on patrol.

> *Dear Family—My weekend in Toronto was quite wearing. I'm afraid my presence upset Peter's mother more than she realized. Then I'd get upset, and by the time I returned to N.Y. I was a mass of knots inside. But I'm glad I went, though I found it hard to return Sunday night with all those dreams of happiness I might have had. Peter had written his mother of what to buy me for Xmas—and in previous letters of things of his he wanted me to have. And so I had to accept so much that I was really embarrassed— it was quite upsetting.*

Bitter thoughts about loved ones we'd lost made our hatred of war sometimes overpowering, in spite of our victory.

Reflecting on IBM's Role

With the war now ended on both fronts, I looked back on the role played by IBM's systems service women, and I had to say they performed their jobs exceptionally well, handling the civilian necessities on the home front as well as keeping the business moving. The corporate growth of IBM during the war period was due in no small way to the efforts of its women employees. What a pity we had no commission plan operating for them at that time.

One systems service woman in the Chicago office, Jacqueline Decker, became IBM's first woman salesperson in 1945. She made her quota and attended the first Hundred Percent Club after the war ended. Other women joined her the following year, working their territories along with the men who were gradually returning to the sales force.

As the fighting men returned home, so did their leaders. Of

the New York City ticker-tape parades I witnessed, General Eisenhower's and General Wainwright's returns from overseas provoked the most emotion. Ike's smile as he sped past the crowds behind the street barriers just about did me in. I shed a tear or two as did the mobs around me that day.

When General Wainwright returned, I remember going into Peck & Peck on Fifth Avenue to ask if I could stand in their display window, a good two and a half feet above the sidewalk and crowds, so I could see the big parade. Most Americans believed there wasn't enough we could do to thank these men for leading us to complete victory.

CHAPTER SIXTEEN

Out of Action

Early in January of 1946, Governor Thomas E. Dewey of New York invited me to serve on his New York State Women's Council, headed by Jane Todd, deputy commissioner of the New York State Department of Commerce. I attended the first meeting, a luncheon in the State house in Albany, presided over by the governor himself, and attended by outstanding women in the fields of education, personnel, labor, the media, and business, as well as by leaders of professional and volunteer groups. My new friend, Elizabeth Arden, sat across from me, pushing her cuticles back while she listened to the governor, just as she had in those Junior Achievement meetings we had both attended.

I had the privilege of sitting to the right of our host, the governor, who said, "Miss Leach, I want you to know that this is a first, a significant landmark in the basic thinking about women in industrial and civic affairs. I hope you and the others around this table will help Jane Todd develop opportunities for women in business and other fields." I reminded him that many people considered Mr. Watson and IBM pioneers in using women in jobs other than secretarial. Unfortunately, I never did work with Miss Todd.

A few weeks later, during the big January sales meeting in Endicott, I sat for hours with a dull pain in my chest that I couldn't really identify. The doctor there thought I had pulled a muscle and he strapped up my chest.

Tom Jr. returned from the Air Force to rejoin the company,

and his father announced at the meeting that he would serve as assistant to Charlie Kirk. The expression on Tom's face didn't really reveal great enthusiasm at that announcement, but we were all glad to have him back in the business.

We also learned the company planned to reorganize the whole sales organization and place it under the direction of Jim Birkenstock from the Kansas City office, who was to become general sales manager. The surprise on Jim's face at Mr. Watson's announcement of his name told us all this was news to him, as it was to all of us. I had forgotten our leader's ability to manipulate his artillery for aiming higher as each year passed, inspiring us all each year to do a better job than the year before.

When I returned from Endicott to New York City, I went to the company doctor, who examined me and took X-rays. I left immediately following that appointment to keep one with the American Council on Education in Washington, where I served on their committee to study what part of Army and Navy military training could be used or applied to civilian education. I felt flattered and pleased to serve with this group.

At home once again, I learned from a lung specialist that I had tuberculosis, which had created a hole in my lung. The timing couldn't have been worse. A few weeks earlier I had learned that the Women's National Press Club planned to honor me for outstanding accomplishment in business. My TB diagnosis came one week before my scheduled trip to Washington for the awards dinner. President Truman was to present the award. My larger-than-life portrait hung with those of the other 10 recipients in the IBM show window at 57th and Madison in New York City. Although this would be the crowning night of my career, my doctor steadfastly refused to let me go.

"But Dr. Riggins, you don't understand. This is a tremendous honor. My family is coming from California to join me at this extremely prestigious affair, which will be attended by the president of the United States and his cabinet. When will I ever receive another award like this from another president? Please, please tell me I can go."

He finally relented, but said, "All right, you can go, but I want you to fly to Washington—not drive or take the train, and stay right at the Mayflower Hotel, where the event will take place. Rest until you go downstairs—to the dinner only. Then return immediately after the ceremony to your room." I didn't follow his orders precisely.

The awards ceremony thrilled me. After making appropriate introductions for each of our awards, President Truman gave his famous speech about the need for Americans to tighten their belts, so we could help feed Europe and get her back on track.

I so enjoyed my dinner companions, too. On my right sat Eugene List, the young pianist who entertained the gathering along with the witty Cornelia Otis Skinner. Next to him sat Margaret Truman. She and List were both closer to my age than anyone else in the room.

Following the huge dinner and important speech, we honorees and others were immediately whisked by the secret service in limousines to Perle Mesta's lovely home for another feast in our honor. No way could we tighten our belts that night! An exceptionally long table filled the equally long sunken dining room, the table piled nearly to the rafters with flower arrangements and food.

An invitation to a gathering from Perle Mesta, the "hostess with the mostest" in the capital, represented the epitome of social acceptance in Washington. We mingled with all the greats of that time on the Washington scene, from General Omar Bradley to whichever ambassadors and European nobility happened to be in town.

Perle Mesta's parties were famous as scenes of political intrigue, and I enjoyed no end standing at the entrance to the sunken dining room, watching Eric Johnston, former head of the U.S. Chamber of Commerce and later with the Hays Office in Hollywood, "working" that enormous room, constantly searching for someone important to talk to. When he reached the far end of the table, he walked very slowly back to where he had started, stopping to mingle with an important guest he'd missed on the way in.

Chester Bowles, IBM's envoy to India, walked across the room to speak to me. "Miss Leach, I want to congratulate you on your award tonight. You certainly have achieved a great success in a very little time. Now, you must tell me, are you really only 29 years old?"

"Yes I am, Mr. Bowles," I replied, " but I've gone through a lot of blood, sweat, and tears to get where I am tonight, and I think I'm aging rapidly."

Later I found myself standing next to General Bradley in a long line waiting to be received by Mrs. Mesta. Not knowing what to say to him, I looked at the array of ribbons on his chest and smiled, "My, but you've been a busy general, sir."

And he replied, "It seems you've been just about as busy in your young life, too."

The following morning my family and I flew back to New York City, where I checked into Doctor's Hospital for a four-month stay to have my lung collapsed so the big hole would heal. No other hospital in that big city would accept me as a tubercular patient, making me feel like a leper who had escaped from Molokai.

My doctor used a treatment called pneumothorax, injecting a pressure of air through a needle into the pleura (lining) against my right lung about every 10 days or two weeks to keep the lung collapsed. At the time (1946), no antibiotics existed to treat tuberculosis, so they kept me on pneumothorax treatments for eight long years until 1953, when I stopped taking the treatments and the lung came up gradually of its own accord, but with much less elasticity than it once had.

Looking back over my life as I lay in my hospital bed, I thought how far I had come in my twenty-nine years—from that innocent, wide-eyed, immature college graduate to a corporate officer at IBM, learning along the way how to roll with the punches—and I'd received my share of them in the corporate world. But I took advantage of all the amazing opportunities and meeting the challenges that came my way.

Above all, I'd loved the excitement of working with and getting to know so many enormously interesting people. The lifetime friendships I made at IBM I still cherish today. I took great satisfaction in watching my unsung heroines blossom as they used their new-found talents in handling their territories as competently as the men they replaced. They really paved the way for women to take on professional and managerial roles in the business world.

Some of my most treasured memories came from taking part in Mr. Watson's fireside discussion groups in his office, particularly the planning for new products and searching for new solutions to problems. If you walk into my living room today, you will find an extra brick beside the fireplace that came from the fireplace in Mr. Watson's office when they tore down the old IBM World Headquarters in New York City. To me, the brick symbolizes all the hours many of us spent around that fireplace, discussing and planning for IBM's role in corporate America and the world.

But there I was, an unhealthy, twenty-nine-year old in a mess, at the peak of a career I had never planned on having. I must have been a feather in the cap of the feminist movement in America, but I didn't even know it.

In Bed

I placed my life in the hands of my TB specialist, Dr. Riggins, a delightful, old-fashioned doctor who really cared about his patients. We often talked at great length about my life and what future I might have. I felt angry and bitter that this debilitating illness happened to me, and I became extremely depressed when I had to stop seeing my then current beau, as much as I wanted him around. I could never give him the family he wanted so badly.

Dr. Riggins suggested that when my hospital sojourn ended, perhaps in May, I return with my mother to the West Coast for further recuperation as New York City wasn't the best place for that. This would mean subletting my apartment, but for how long?

I laugh now when I think about being admitted to Doctors Hospital in New York. The registrar said, "Would you like to have a $17 a day room facing west into the tenements (complete with laundry strewn between the buildings) or an $18 a day room with a view of the East River?" At the time, I considered that an outrageous price. IBM had no hospitalization program then, so most of my salary seemed to go toward my medical bills.

Mr. and Mrs. Watson visited me often, which I appreciated very much. They wanted me to keep my illness to myself and not reveal the nature of my problem to anyone. My mother, who stayed in my apartment during my hospital sojourn and tended to my needs, told me that attitude toward TB had been common in her youth. She remembered heavy whispers about "consumption," which was dangerously contagious and therefore rarely discussed openly. I guess Mr. Watson didn't want to unleash a panic in IBM that I might have spread contamination through the company.

Some weeks later my father, who stayed in San Francisco during my hospital stay, somehow heard rumors questioning whether I was ill or pregnant and just sitting life out until "my time" came. He did not like what he heard, so he picked up the telephone and called Mr. Phillips, then executive vice president at IBM, and asked that he please put an end to this kind of talk.

After six weeks in the hospital without a single piece of mail, I suddenly received bags of mail daily, to say nothing of the flowers and plants that came in from all over the country. My picture appeared on the front page of IBM's weekly news sheet bordered with a black line, telling where I was and why, with the hospital's address in case anyone should want to write me. When I saw all that black around my picture, I thought perhaps I had died.

The hospital mailroom and the receptionist on my floor wanted to know who on earth I was to be receiving such mail. I never knew I had so many friends. Also, every IBM office had an "IBM Club" whose secretary usually attended to sending cards on behalf of her office to the sick, the newly married, or to IBM widows. That upped the volume considerably. But I felt flattered and appreciated all my fan mail at a time when my spirits had sunk pretty low.

On one of Mr. Watson's visits he said, "Now Miss Leach, you must get well by June so you can go to Hartwick College in Oneonta, NY, to accept an honorary degree from them." I appreciated his trying to help me think optimistically about my recovery, but his schedule seemed a little over-sanguine.

Life in a hospital wasn't all that bad if you took a positive attitude toward living there. I managed to learn about the background of the nurses on my floor and became good friends with them all, to the point that they would come in during their break to have a cigarette and a chat. Often, when the head nurse came looking for them, they would hurry from the room, leaving me holding their lit cigarettes in either hand—and I obviously had no business smoking in my predicament!

Then there were the celebrities, such as Spencer Tracy in the next room "drying out." I kept trying the old glass-against-the-wall trick to listen through to his room, hoping for some juicy conversations. Aside from all that, I read every book on the bestseller list, fiction and non-fiction, during the spring of 1946—a feat I don't recommend and one I'll probably never again attempt in my lifetime.

At the end of April, Charlie Kirk and his wife, Mildred, came to see me. Charlie said, "We've been talking about you at the office, and we want to reimburse you for all the medical expenses you've incurred here." I suddenly felt responsible for some new hospitalization program that IBM planned to instigate. But I appreciated their decision so much that I broke down and cried right in front of Charlie and his wife. Physically, I felt so weak I just couldn't help myself. I had worried about my future and where I would fit in, or really, what might become of me? I just knew nobody would employ me with my TB record, and that no man would want to marry me in my unhealthy state.

But dear Charlie said, "I want to reassure you, Ruth, that after you recuperate for a year or so, we will always have a place for you in IBM." I needed that reassurance so badly.

Finally, after three and a half months, with my mother beside me, Dr. Riggins released me to return home to my apartment to spend the month of May—still recuperating, but learning to spend part of each day up moving around to strengthen my muscles and start walking again. By the end of May I could walk one block to the end of East 73rd Street by Central Park. After another week, I was walking inside the park via the East 72nd Street entrance to a bench beside a little lake nearby where I enjoyed watching children sail their boats and squirrels prancing down the trees.

Sometimes Nancy Watson, Dick's wife, and I would meet and walk in the park with their firstborn Ann in the pram. It was the only way Nancy could spend time alone with her own baby away from the scrutiny of the bossy, elderly Watson family nanny. We did enjoy our Central Park excursions together and watching spring "busting out all over." I found this a peaceful and relaxing way of life that I hadn't known for years.

Jack and Helen Kenney solved my subleasing problem by deciding to rent my apartment while I was away. Having said grateful goodbyes to so many faithful friends, I felt prepared for the long train ride home to California to recuperate.

On my day of departure from New York, Tom Jr. sent me one of those huge bon voyage baskets with all kinds of fruit for the train trip home. I had to use a wheelchair to get through Penn Station to the train during a time when there was a troop movement, of all things, and how fitting! The army must have decided I needed a good sendoff: they lined up on either side of mother and me, and a porter wheeled me to the train through a tunnel of soldiers, my lap piled high with the huge fruit basket, mother's train case, our books and handbags. Everyone thought I must be some celebrity, but they weren't sure. I blew a kiss back to "my boys" and left New York City to embark on what turned out to be more than a year of recuperation.

Since my sister and brother-in-law had moved with their two small children into an old roomy house in Piedmont, I had planned on staying with them instead of with my parents who had just sold their home and moved to a small apartment. But my doctor strongly urged me not to live with young children about, as tuberculosis was highly contagious, particularly to them. After a week or so, my mother fell ill and became unable to cope with my routine, nor could I cope with hers. So I decided to leave and continue my recuperation at a small resort, Robles del Rio Lodge in Carmel Valley about one hundred miles from Oakland. Located near enough for family and friends to visit me, it provided restful quiet for the kind of life I had to lead.

Each time my father came to visit he would present me with another kit to make a boat, a cable car, a plane, and other models, and I made new friends as I sat by the pool under a huge oak tree putting together my project during my "play" time. I spent an enjoyable six months of quiet living, resting and dining with new friends at the lodge, or playing backgammon or dominoes around the pool.

The season closed November 30th and back I came to Piedmont, but this time to my sister's. We decided we could keep the children away from me by making a game of it.

Tom Watson Jr. came by for tea one afternoon while in San Francisco on business, and Mary Schultz spent a weekend and we had a nice visit. But, so many of my friends kept busy with their young families and volunteer work that I hardly saw them. As Christmas neared, everyone except me seemed terribly busy. The world kept spinning, and everyone else's life seemed so very exciting, but I didn't feel a part of it. The gloomy weather made me feel even gloomier.

Plus, I disliked being a burden to my family after having been so independent for years.

Look on the Sunny Side

I made a decision. If I had to sit life out, why not do so out in the sunshine. So I called Henry Owen, the IBM manager of the Phoenix office, and asked him if he might find me some accommodations for about six months after the holidays.

On January 2, 1947, I stepped off the train in Phoenix and viewed a stark desert with a treeless horizon. "What an expanse of nothingness," I thought. "How can I stand six months of this?"

Mr. Owen met me at the train and drove me out to nearby Scottsdale, a real western town then with dirt roads and Indian squaws sitting on the dirt sidewalks making leather handbags for Lloyd Kiva, a famous Indian craftsman. Wyatt Earp-type characters loped into town on their quarter horses and tied them up beside the swinging doors of the local corner saloon. About a mile from this scene stood the Jokake Inn where I planned to live for the next few months.

As the days passed and I became stronger, my surroundings

began to grow on me. I couldn't yet ride horseback, but I enjoyed watching the trick riders practice and the cowboys develop their roping skills.

One day I learned the crown prince of Saudi Arabia was coming to visit the desert and the U.S. State Department had selected Jokake Inn for his stay in the area. I happened to be sitting in the front office when the manager spoke of his anxiety over the Prince's visit. I offered my help, and made several suggestions based on my IBM experience like: flying the Saudi flag during his stay, placing the fruits of the desert as well as a queen-size bed in his room, providing a proper Saudi Arabian diet, and other ideas. I felt delighted I could help.

Mr. and Mrs. Watson visited the IBM office in Phoenix during my stay. By telephone, I helped Mr. Owen make luncheon arrangements, since it was Mr. Watson's birthday that day. Then, I managed to borrow a friend's car and attend the gathering.

By the end of April, when Jokake Inn closed for its season, I had become fully acclimated to the desert and loved every aspect of it. I enjoyed my visit there so much, I promised myself I'd return every year for my holiday. I had made lasting friendships there, and hated to leave. But I also couldn't wait to return to IBM in New York and go back to work on a part-time basis. I'd been too idle for too long and wanted to get on with some kind of life again. Besides, I was nearly broke.

A lung specialist in San Francisco administered my pneumothorax treatments every two weeks when I stayed in Carmel Valley. In Phoenix another TB specialist took care of me. But I was anxious to return to Dr. Riggins and learn what progress I had made in healing that hole in my lung.

CHAPTER SEVENTEEN

IBM Women Betrayed...and Where Do I Fit In?

When I finally returned to New York in the summer of 1947, the pace of life seemed so much busier than a year and a half before when I'd left for California. Or perhaps the contrast to the pastoral life I'd led out West made it seem that way. Foreigners filled the city, and strange sounding languages rang in my ears as I walked down Madison Avenue.

Though many new faces greeted me at World Headquarters, those who knew me welcomed me with great warmth. I had my old office back on the 16th floor, next to Tom Jr. and across from Al Williams, the top financial officer at that time.

Mr. Watson Sr. wanted me to work part-time for awhile, so he set my work hours from 10:30 a.m. until 3:30 p.m. He even ordered a black leather psychiatrist's couch for my office so I could take a "quiet hour" if needed. He really pampered me, fearing for my health and afraid I might overdo. Maybe, too, I reminded him of what happens when a job places too much stress on a person.

Roy Stephens and "Army" Armstrong, who had recently retired from IBM, took me to lunch my first day back, as did other executives on subsequent days. They each spent time bringing me up to date on what had gone on in the company during my absence.

Jeanne Cotten, my roommate from our 1939 systems service class served as personnel manager at 590, as we called World Headquarters when it was located at 590 Madison Avenue in New York City. During my absence Jeanne and Jane Haislip had worked on solving the problem of what to do with all the young women we had hired now that the men had begun returning from the war. Some of these women went into IBM sales and became very successful at it, and normal attrition took care of many others, who married and left the company. But that apparently wasn't good enough.

Just after the war ended, IBM instituted a policy that married women could no longer work for the company. Management immediately released those women already married, with no severance pay. From that point on, if a woman employee married she had to resign. Mr. Watson felt that married women belonged at home, at the center of family life.

He did make exceptions for some special hardship cases, women who served as breadwinners for their families, putting husbands through law school or medical school, for example. But he rarely strayed from the policy, and for the most part, married women had to leave IBM and find employment elsewhere. The company even denied one woman a big promotion because she was planning to marry. She told me if she had known about the promotion, she probably would have delayed her marriage or concealed it altogether. Some women did keep their marriages a secret so they could continue working. Can you imagine women in today's workplace tolerating conditions like those?

This policy proved a bitter pill to swallow. For years the company applauded the IBM women for protecting and even increasing the revenue of the company during the war years, and for doing such a fine job of keeping IBM's customers well satisfied with our service. But 1946 and 1947 changed that. Those must have been dreary years for IBM women when the company began treating them as second class citizens. Jane Haislip and Jeanne Cotten both confessed much later that those were the cruelest times they had spent in all their days at IBM.

Because of my convalescence I missed those times, and didn't learn about the policy until my return because no one wanted to burden me with her problems. Everyone seemed to consider me a casualty of sorts already, and they felt I had enough to cope with just trying to regain my health. When I finally returned to work and learned what had happened, I couldn't believe it. By that time, Mr. Watson Sr.'s "married woman" policy had already been in operation for a year, and everyone considered it his way of solving the problem of too many women in the sales department.

We women really felt betrayed. However, with few exceptions, the systems service women, though outraged, accepted the policy as a rule they had to follow. I guess we acted like sheep. But at that time women felt grateful for the superb opportunities IBM had given them, the best in the nation then, and they loved their jobs while they lasted. At least IBM prepared women for other, perhaps better, opportunities later.

Adding Further Insult

Recruiting women for systems service work came to a standstill during the adjustment months. The well-seasoned women still employed by IBM to teach the newly hired men and retrain IBM salesmen returning from the war, found that the male students they taught earned three to four times more than they did. That women have always been paid less than men for comparable work was and continues to be a bone of contention, even up through the executive ranks. But I could hardly complain about salary when the company had paid all my hospital and medical bills for a year and a half plus my full salary during my leave of absence. In fact, my contracting tuberculosis improved the lot of all IBM employees, as my hospital experience served as the beginning of IBM's hospitalization program.

Despite Mr. Watson's restrictions, it seemed as if just about everyone got married anyway during those years just after the war. Jeanne, Jane and I often laughed secretly at the remarks made by some of the veterans returning to IBM who had known us before.

"Hi, girls. You're still such an attractive trio, why aren't you all married yet?" they'd joke.

We'd reply "No one's invited us," or " We've been so busy, we haven't had the time," or whatever came to our minds. It seemed that these men, away from the workplace so long, had retained the old-fashioned assumption that all women were "girls," to be valued chiefly for procreation and care-giving. They had no idea what we had done in IBM during their absence.

I have to admit, though, that annoying as they were, we felt a bit let down when the wisecracks stopped after a few weeks' bombardment. One day, Jeanne asked if any of the men still asked me those silly questions. "Maybe they don't think we're as attractive as we used to be," she said. Sexual harassment circa 1947: they were putting us in our place, they thought.

Finding My Niche

After all my travels before and during the war, I never thought I'd feel happy to step on a train again. But when Vin Learson, the new sales manager and shining star of Tom Jr.'s new team asked me to visit the Philadelphia and Washington, DC, offices, I accepted with delight and anticipation. Learson, later to become president of IBM, wanted me to interview some salesmen about their new approach to selling IBM products. Instead of specializing in just one area, these men sold all the products of IBM's three divisions: accounting machines, time-recording equipment, and electric typewriters. I was to determine: did those salesmen like selling the entire line? Did they find it more economical to sell that way? And, what was their experience?

From the Northeast, I continued on to the Midwest and interviewed more salesmen selling the whole line of products. Based on my interviews, we concluded that those salesmen with sales territories heavily populated with companies that could use large accounting installations should concentrate on selling only accounting machines to prospects. This method provided far more profit for the company as well as for the salesmen, but it took longer to sell that way.

Selling typewriters to a prospect took less time than selling an accounting system, but the profit wasn't as great. The salesman had to contact many prospects each day to make his quota. In certain territories, however, where prospects were widespread, three-way selling did save time and made for greater profits.

Returning home, I marched down to Mr. Learson's office to hand him the results of my interviews, feeling happy about doing something constructive and more confident of myself than I'd felt for some time.

"Oh, you can keep that," he said brushing me off, "I had someone else do it for me." If I had had another job to go to, I would have left IBM at that moment, after first telling the new sales manager what I thought of him. What a waste of IBM's time and money. So much for my admiration of the cruel Mr. Learson. I knew as long as he headed sales, I could have no part of it. I would not work with him again, nor would I go out on Christmas Eve as he requested each year, to buy a gift for his wife. The big question was: if not in sales, what could I do in IBM in my fragile physical state?

The answer, at least in Mr. Watson's mind, seemed to be public relations. Judging from the assignments he now gave me, he seemed to want me to represent IBM as an executive at all sorts of gatherings: to serve on committees in the community, attend ribbon-cutting ceremonies, entertain VIPs nationally or internationally for IBM. Over the next few years, I also served on several local boards such as: the National Camp Fire Girls, Inc., the New York Tuberculosis and Health Board, the Women's Board of the New York Public Library, the Metropolitan Opera Guild, and many others. Though never officially given a goal, my purpose in all this seemed to be projecting the right image of IBM to the community, a task that neither Mr. Watson nor Tom had time for in those busy early years of building an IBM computer world. I really didn't mind the job at all. Plus, my varied assignments led to some interesting experiences.

An especially memorable event took place one Saturday as Jane Haislip and I prepared to go to Endicott for a week. When Mr. Watson asked us to represent IBM at the dedication of New

York's new Idyllwild Airport out on Long Island, later renamed the JFK International Airport, we resented having to give up a lovely Saturday to attend. But the day turned out to be more exciting than we could have imagined.

The event started with a big luncheon at the Waldorf attended by lots of VIPs. As each guest arrived, a New York City fireman in full dress complete with white gloves, escorted him or her to a reserved table. Then the best Irish tenors that the New York City Police Department had to offer entertained us all. Nowhere but in New York City could you find such a scene.

The master of ceremonies announced there would be no after-lunch speeches and, true to his word, immediately following lunch he directed us all out the right exit to board buses for a ride to Idyllwild. Motorcade-style, complete with police escorts, flags and lots of sirens, we paraded our way through the city. What a thrill!

We all hurried to our reserved seats to view the next scene: Air Force One landed in front of us and President Truman stepped out and was escorted to our platform area by motorcycle police, holding huge banners instead of swords, walking on either side of his open limousine. Above us, four groups of B-17 planes, each having flown in formation from either Seattle, San Diego, Texas or Florida, each arrived on time, in succession, an example of true Army Air Force logistics.

In spite of not wanting to go in the first place, Jane and I felt moved by all of the pageantry and reveled in the joy of being out on such a gloriously beautiful day.

The Joys of Fundraising

In the fall of 1949 when Mr. Watson volunteered my services to Mrs. August Belmont as treasurer of the first Metropolitan Opera fund drive, I never could have imagined the number of social aspects the assignment would involve. Mrs. Belmont really wanted Tom Jr. on her committee, but his busy schedule organizing IBM's first steps into the computer world kept him from participating.

The Met's goal, to raise $250,000, seems modest by today's

standards, but in 1949 that sum seemed tremendous. We promoted the fund drive through social functions featuring current or recently retired opera stars. Lauder Greenway, president of the Metropolitan Opera Board, generously hosted small dinner parties at Pavillion, one of New York's exclusive restaurants and the "in" place to be seen and heard. I felt very out of place in this snobbish atmosphere, but if we impressed our would-be donors, so be it. I actually had fun watching Greta Garbo at the next table, listening to Cole Porter who sat behind me at one function, and sharing a table with Lucretia Bori and Guiseppe De Luca.

Some of the fundraising events seemed downright bizarre, like the cocktail party at opera singer Stella Roman's apartment. She had filled the place with rare birds all flying loose everywhere and we kept checking each other's head and shoulders in case we needed a clean-up job. Her numerous glass cabinets displayed Oriental vials containing water from every sea of the world. But our guests seemed to enjoy these parties and they did help us to achieve our goal.

My escort to these affairs was my so-called assistant, a handsome young man on the board of Met's Opera Guild. He seemed quite the ladies' man and took care of Mrs. Belmont's widowed friends at opera functions. We enjoyed each other's senses of humor and had fun entertaining the opera donors. Then our friendship became more serious to him than to me, and the next thing I knew he had presented me with a two-carat diamond ring which I regretfully returned, explaining I just didn't care for him in the same way he seemed to care for me.

As treasurer for the opera fund drive, I set up a simple accounting system on punched cards, one card for each donor with the donor's name and address, phone number, amount of contribution and other pertinent information needed. An IBM accounting machine, the 405 machine (circa 1949), was wired to pick up the information punched in the cards and print it in a designated place on paper. All monies that came in were handled by me and deposited in a special bank account. We also handled newspaper coverage of the Fund Drive with appropriate photos. The most time-consuming job, however, was approaching donor prospects on a one-to-one basis. Finally, one evening I found myself on the opera house stage during an intermission, presenting a check to Mr. Greenway for more than $250,000. Mission accomplished.

I felt more at home on the national board of the Campfire Girls. As the only member of the board who had been a Campfire Girl, a camper as well as a counselor, I was put on the camping committee. In that capacity, I got to visit some summer camps in upstate New York and in California the next summer, sleeping in their infirmaries and making suggestions and evaluations of each camp in my report.

I soon found out that in fundraising it's who you know and how you approach them that counts. I went to see Mrs. Bernard F. Gimbel, a fellow member of the board, who in turn introduced me to Marshall Field and Dorothy Shaver, president of Lord and Taylor's in New York. All these people appreciated how much time IBM employees gave to help the various non-profit organizations in New York City, and that was certainly good public relations for our company.

I also became a member of the Women's Council of the New York Public Library and felt bowled over when they gave us a tour of the seven floors of stacks—eighty-five miles of books—at the New York Public Library. We lunched with the chairman of the board of the library, Morris Hadley, who gave us our orders regarding fundraising and its importance to the City of New York.

The New York Tuberculosis and Health Association also invited me to join their group, primarily to educate the public on the hazards of this dreaded disease. I certainly could identify with their mission, and I really enjoyed doing radio work for them in their campaign to get their message across to the public.

So, my job assignments had changed considerably, and from a health standpoint, as long as I avoided any stress in my life, I felt content to accept any "human relations" assignment they gave me. In fact, I began to feel like the IBM poster girl.

CHAPTER EIGHTEEN

Executive Moves and Banquets by the Week

A series of tragedies struck IBM beginning in June of 1947. Charlie Kirk, IBM's executive vice president, died suddenly of a heart attack in Lyons, France, while on a business trip with Tom Jr. We had a huge funeral in Endicott and Mr. Watson led the mourners. Then three months later Vice President Fred Nichol, who had not been around at all since my return, made formal his resignation because of ill health. And the following month Roy Stephens also died unexpectedly of a heart attack. I began to consider the danger of being a vice president of IBM and felt pretty fortunate to have gotten away with just a case of TB Mr. Watson, though a giant of a man, put tremendous pressure on his executives, and it proved too much for some of us.

Executive Moves

In the mid-Forties, a series of executive personnel changes came as no great surprise to anyone. Tom Jr. became a vice president; Mr. Phillips, an executive vice president; and Al Williams treasurer of the company. Tom also joined the executive and finance committees of the board. I offered to trade offices with Tom as I had a larger one in a corner of the 16th floor just under his dad's office on the 17th floor. But he wouldn't have it. Mr. Watson Sr. wanted to expose Tom to all aspects of the business as soon as possible, and we all could see the game of checkers being played to move Tom forward square by square, jumping over others in the way.

During this time, Tom Jr. began pushing for IBM to manufacture an electronic calculator, which several large IBM customers had virtually demanded. Jim Birkenstock kept telling Tom that punched cards were a thing of the past and that our customers wanted more speed. We began losing money and customers to UNIVAC. The biggest obstacle to beginning production of this calculator was selling Tom's father on that idea.

Those of us on the 16th floor could see the ping pong game going on between father and son. But Tom persevered, insisting that IBM must come up with a machine that would out-perform Remington Rand's UNIVAC. He hired many electronic engineers and put an MIT engineering graduate whom his father liked in charge. They worked day and night and by January 1948 (within two years) IBM dedicated the Selective Sequence Electronic Calculator, (SSEC). The SSEC worked much faster than the ASCC, the automatic sequence controlled calculator, which IBM built during the war and presented to Harvard for wartime use.

Mr. Watson Sr. hated to give up the punched card machines, so he called this new machine IBM's "first electronic computer for scientific research." He could not imagine anyone using computers for accounting, though in time Tom convinced him that the computer represented the future for IBM.

The company installed the SSEC on the ground floor of World Headquarters at 57th and Madison, so everyone walking by could watch it operate. For demonstration purposes our engineers set it up to project the position of the moon in space at any given time, which involved performing many mathematical equations. But its primary use was to solve problems in pure science or other non-profitable mathematical cases. It had some problems, however, and proved to be slower than expected. So, Tom Jr. directed a new set of engineers to build an all electronic machine to be called the "Defense Calculator," or the 701.

Right before the unveiling of the SSEC, Mr. Watson gave a large luncheon for over 125 of the country's leading scientists, mathematicians, and physicists, along with New York City notables, such as Nelson Rockefeller, Jim Farley, David Sarnoff, head of RCA, and the heads of AT&T, General Electric and other companies. William Shockley, the inventor of the transistor, and John von Neumann, the computer theorist, also attended. The guest of honor was J. Robert Oppenheimer, the great physicist who directed the building of the first atom bomb, who in his talk complimented IBM on this great event (the development of the SSEC) as a giant step for all mankind.

One noted mathematician attending from the Bureau of Standards in Washington, D.C., was a woman, the only one on the guest list, and Mr. Watson thought she should not be a lone female in an audience of men, so at the last minute he included Mrs. Watson and me.

As master of ceremonies, Mr. Watson first introduced the members at the long head table. When it came time to introduce the female mathematician he also introduced Mrs. Watson as "the scientist in our family, and Miss Leach, IBM vice president, who is in the audience and works in science, too." My IBM buddies who were present began to snicker quietly, and I looked hard down at my napkin. I never had an introduction quite like that, nor could I explain what I did "in science."

Steering Toward Success

It soon became clear that Tom Jr. planned to steer the company well into the computer world. Five years after the company introduced the SSEC, which had been used solely for scientific work, IBM brought out the faster, more profitable smaller machine, 701, developed for customers to use in their offices. The 701 replaced the now-obsolete SSEC on the ground floor of World Headquarters.

Tom's foresight paved the way for IBM to become the corporate giant we know today, but Mr. Watson Sr. was the true salesman in the family. No wonder America considered him the greatest salesman in the business world. And he sold the IBM image better than anything else. I always loved the words Tom Jr. used to describe his father's sales ability: "At the New York World's Fair of 1939, there was a General Motors Day, a General Electric Day, and an IBM Day—two elephants and a gnat all getting the same treatment." No one ever dreamed we were as small a company as we really were in those pre-war days. But thanks to Tom during his "golden years" when he took over the reins from his father and entered headlong the unknown world of computers, IBM, the gnat, surpassed in size the two elephants, General Motors and General Electric.

Celebrating Successes

In mid-August of 1947 the largest Hundred Percent Club in IBM's history convened in Endicott to honor the salesmen who had reached one hundred percent of their respective quotas that year. It was my first big convention, and like the hordes of journalists and photographers in attendance, I felt duly impressed with the awesome scene IBM had constructed on the Homestead grounds.

Workers had enlarged Tent City and moved it up into the park, out of sight from the Homestead. The new structures housed the 1,200 or so salesmen. The "main tent," or "big top," erected on the parking lot, was a huge circus tent complete with platform, banners, blown-up photos of the sales leaders, microphones, lights, several fans to combat the hot humid weather, and fifteen hundred chairs. At the publishing tent we printed a daily paper with pictures and speeches from the previous day. The company had also set up a reception tent that held a display of various IBM machines; an administrative tent; a boot black and laundry tent; and a Coca-Cola tent where the crowd consumed over twenty thousand bottles of sodas in three and a half days.

Everyone convened in the main tent each morning at 8:30, and the speeches went on until 1:00. After lunch most of the group played sports all afternoon then attended banquets each evening.

Jane, Jeanne, Helen Taft and I served as greeters. For two days we, and several sales executives, welcomed train car loads of IBM qualifiers for the Hundred Percent Club from all over the world. I loved greeting old friends I had not seen for some time.

The first evening's banquet, held at the IBM Country Club down the hill from the Homestead, featured the graduation of a sales class with all twelve hundred "Hundred Percenters" assembled. I sat on the dais next to Dick Watson, who made his first speech in IBM as president of the graduating sales class that night. When dinner started, he hadn't yet written a word of it , and he felt terribly nervous about performing in front of his father, so I helped him draft something while we ate. We both sighed with relief when he finished, and despite his nervousness, the presentation turned out quite well.

The following morning Mr. Watson opened the "Club" convention by introducing all the IBM directors and officers assembled on the platform. Then came speech after speech from the Hundred Percent Club officers, interspersed with talks by the sales manager and other officers of the company. The heat and humidity made sitting inside that big tent almost unbearable. Everyone quickly soaked through their full business attire, and we could hardly wait for lunch so we could return to our respective rooms to undress and cool off.

That evening's banquet, a huge tribute dinner in honor of Mr. Watson's third of a century with IBM, was by far the biggest affair of its kind the company had ever undertaken—a good fifteen hundred or more attended. Large speakers piped the festivities, which lasted well past midnight, all over the golf course where hundreds of people who couldn't get into the big tent sat. Each department gave speeches and presented gifts to Mr. Watson: the board of directors, the manufacturing organization, the field sales offices, World Headquarters, and the World Trade division.

My speech came at the very end, as I was designated to present a gift to Mrs. Watson—a solid gold Cartier picture frame the size of a compact that extended to hold four snapshots of her four children. The tricky part was to give that lovely lady her due without drawing attention away from her husband, who ate up the accolades heaped on him by all the speakers that evening. He loved these affairs and the attention given to him. So I worked hard over that speech, and I think I managed to strike the right note.

After paying tribute to the honored guest on his night of nights, I added, "If I were a painter and someone asked me to paint a portrait of Mr. Watson, I would not paint him against an international background, nor would I paint him in his New York office, nor against any other of the many fields in which he is interested. I would paint him against the background of Endicott, the plant, the laboratory and the schoolhouse—the heart of IBM, where he pioneered a type of industrialism that is today admired and respected the world over. It was in Endicott where the seed of his long constructive career was planted and nurtured.

"But even then, and I'm sure you will agree with me, this portrait against such a background would not be complete without something else, Mr. Watson's greatest asset, Mrs. Watson. In so many of the things in which he has participated she has stood by his side, traveling all over the world, over hundreds of thousands of miles. And in her quiet gracious manner she has charmed everyone with whom she came in contact, whether in the IBM offices and plants or among kings and princes.

"On behalf of all the women of our organization I would like to pay my tribute to you, Mr. Watson, not only for the many opportunities you have given us in IBM, but for giving us Mrs. Watson as our first lady, our inspiration and our ideal.

"We are particularly proud and grateful knowing that you will share with her the honors which have been bestowed on you tonight. To you, Mrs. Watson, I would like to present on this memorable occasion a token of our gratitude and appreciation for your loyalty, your understanding, your direct contributions to this organization, and for your indirect contributions as a wife and mother, and the very important part you have played in your husband's career. It is my privilege to pay tribute to you, Mrs. Watson, as well as to Mr. Watson tonight."

The presentation moved both her and Mr. Watson visibly. For once, he couldn't even talk! And I had felt so nervous I just knew I had collapsed my other lung. At the end of the evening, Jack

Kenney and others told me it was the best delivered speech of the whole night and the best one I'd ever made. Jack said, "Ruth, you should have a raise after that one." At least I knew the kind of talk "T.J." liked, but I wasn't sure Tom Jr. appreciated all the fanfare bestowed on his father. I felt certain when he finally came to power, all that flattering talk would end.

The final banquet on Friday showcased that year's "Hundred Percenters"—including the first six women ever honored. Each member received his or her congratulatory letter along with a check for excellent work the previous year.

The magazine writers and photographers who attended were impressed by the tremendous amount of organization required to handle the crowds all week: transporting them here and there, creating seating lists for each banquet, and presenting such good food for so many people each night. Mr. Watson loved putting on this kind of show.

I felt happy to be in Endicott that week, for the first time free of any responsibility whatsoever.

Honoring Fallen Heros

Saturday morning the convention closed with more speeches, goodbyes and thank-yous. At 11 a.m. the employees of the plant dedicated a memorial to IBM's war dead—114 men and one woman. Once again I sat on the speaker's stand, with General Maxwell Taylor, head of West Point, and Commodore Tobin of the Navy, both of whom made fitting tributes to those IBMers who made the supreme sacrifice.

Mr. Watson then gave a luncheon for all the relatives of the IBMers who had died. The gesture impressed all of those who attended, and they particularly enjoyed meeting the general and the commodore, and dining at the Homestead. I sat between a postman whose IBM son was killed and a policeman from Johnson City, NY, whose brother was a drill press operator before his death. All in all, some 5,600 IBMers served in the armed forces during World War II—209 of them women. More than ninety percent of those who served returned to the company after the war.

The long week took its toll on me. Despite my resting all afternoon away from the heat of the day, seven days of sitting through meetings every morning and banquets half the night really got to me. Physically I wasn't ready for this kind of "work," and I began to wonder now if working for IBM would prove too much for the state of my health. And I couldn't help wondering just where I would fit in this new world?

By the time the convention ended I felt exhausted. Just the thought of hearing another speech made me want to scream. Tom Jr. told me to take the next week off to rest, and as Labor Day was the following weekend, I flew to Cincinnati for a long visit with some old friends. The weather turned much cooler, and I napped each day, so the circles under my eyes disappeared, and I began to look almost healthy again.

We Liked Ike...and Other Celebs

IBM always made a big deal about its Hundred Percent Club conventions, putting on a big show and inviting special guest speakers. At the 1948 convention, General Dwight D. ("Ike") Eisenhower delighted us all with his off-the-cuff remarks. It was an election year and both the Democrats and the Republicans wanted him on their ticket...and where was he? In Endicott with us! Later, when he became president and was forced to deliver his speeches from written notes, I felt he lacked the eloquence he'd shown that night at our convention dinner.

Mr. Watson asked me to address the group on the same day as the general spoke, so I brought out an old speech I had made a few years before to a sales graduating class. T.J. considered it a good one the first time around, so why not recycle it? Jarmila Novotna, the Metropolitan Opera star, sang at the banquet that evening, and I escorted her to all the festivities planned so she wouldn't get lost. She was such a charmer and a delightful person that I was happy to be her guide.

As long as Mr. Watson headed IBM, we knew we would have pageantry at any and all of the company's gatherings. We had great fun rubbing elbows with the rich and famous during those years. At the 1949 sales convention in Endicott, for example, we presented General of the Army George C. Marshall as our special guest. In 1919, General John J. Pershing called Marshall the "best officer in the U.S. Army." As Chief of Staff of the Army, Marshall established a reputation for brilliance. Following World War II, people throughout Europe were starving and in despair, fighting Communism on all sides. As Secretary of State, Marshall wrote the Truman Doctrine, later renamed the Marshall Plan, which called for the United States to help feed the starving people in war-ravaged Europe. By doing this, the United States took a leadership role in the world and also gained an upper hand over Communism. Marshall was the great statesman who demanded justice for the people of the world, and got it.

Mr. Watson asked me to join the group greeting General Marshall at the airport, then sent me back to where I was staying to get a hat to wear. It never occurred to me on a hot, humid July day in the country to dress up complete with hat and gloves, but I guess our leader wanted us to make an impression on our guest.

At the opening session honoring eighteen hundred top IBM salesmen, there were the usual introductions and speeches. After lunch the session reconvened to introduce eight new IBM machines. When the general, who sat next to me at lunch, asked me to explain the machines, my heart sank. Not having been in sales to learn about the new products coming along, I felt lost, and embarrassed that I hadn't boned up on them beforehand.

The next day, I sat on the platform with the fifteen or twenty sales executives being honored. We were joined by Mr. Watson, General Marshall, a Mr. Kleitz, president of the Guaranty Trust Bank, who sat at my left, and a Mr. Stone, vice president of Prudential Life Insurance, on my right. IBM had just borrowed an unheard of eighty-five million dollars from Prudential, at that time the largest single sum ever borrowed from an insurance company.

After hearing talks from Messieurs Kleitz and Stone, Mr. Watson decided I should say something. Taken totally by surprise, I began to feel a little sick. Stuck to the chair in a cold sweat, I feared I wouldn't be able to make a sound my throat was so dry.

At a time like that, I always thanked Mr. Watson for bringing to us his many distinguished friends—eminent statesmen and successful businessmen, and others. Then I said, "I know of no other position on a platform so enviable as the one I have had this morning—surrounded by all that MONEY—with Guaranty Trust on one side of me and Prudential Insurance on the other...."

My ad-libbing brought down the house, so I quickly sat down while the laughter continued. Even the general, who was the next speaker, got up and commented on that one. It seemed to please Mr. Watson that our guests enjoyed such a good laugh on me.

That evening, Mr. Watson gave a private dinner party for the general at the Homestead prior to what must have been the biggest fireworks show on earth. I wrote to my family and described the magnificent event in honor of General Marshall:

Dear Family—What a night we had! Workers roped off the two golf fairways behind the Endicott Country Club for the festivities, and placed 30,000 chairs in front of a huge platform erected just for the occasion. Everybody prayed there wouldn't be a funeral in any of the neighboring towns as we had rented all the funeral parlor chairs. Even so, about 5,000 people stood during the entire evening. You can imagine what a tremendous undertaking this was, with all the men used to transport people, police the crowds, and light up this huge affair.

Gladys Swarthout and Lawrence Tibbett sang off-key, and General Marshall reminisced about his army career, speaking generally (!) about the importance of morale. It was so hot on that platform that all of us had to shield our faces from the lights. Each light was a 10,000-watt bulb, and there were a good dozen of them on either side of the platform, to say nothing of the terrifically strong footlights, which attracted an enormous amount of bugs. Everyone collected them in their ears, down their necks, and in their hair. We were afraid to open our mouths for fear of swallowing them, and we wondered how the speakers fared that night.

Following the program, the company presented a fireworks spectacle, the likes of which you have never seen. It went on for a long time, and the finale, as you might guess, was a wall of fireworks in many colors spelling out the word THINK, of course.

This was pageantry with a capital "P," and I'm sure the citizens of the entire valley talked about General Marshall's evening for many months afterwards.

CHAPTER NINETEEN

Life with the Inimitable Mr. Watson, Sr.

In the early years of building the European business, Mr. Watson sought out the most intelligent aristocrats to head IBM operations in each country. Thus, the landed gentry became part of the IBM leadership in Europe. Mr. Watson also worked hard to strike up friendships with the influential nobility of Europe, which was facilitated by his position as president of the International Chamber of Commerce.

One summer, when Mr. Watson visited the IBM office in London during his usual European trip, he was amazed to learn that William Howard, a dignified magistrate and member of the British IBM board, had never visited America. Mr. Watson immediately booked him passage to New York, then wired Tom Jr. to make sure that Mr. Howard saw everything he wanted to see as "our guest."

Tom and I met Mr. Howard at the ship and took him to lunch at the Waldorf Starlight Roof, not knowing the restaurant planned to present an elegant fashion show featuring backless dresses and some necklines down to "there." In his charming British accent Mr. Howard kept muttering, "My word, how extraordinary!" He couldn't keep his eyes off of the pretty models. Maybe he'd never seen a fashion show before.

Tom told him, "Now, Mr. Howard, Miss Leach will be your

social chairman during your visit to America. So you tell her what you want to see, and she will arrange everything."

This assignment became much more than I had planned for and lasted much longer than I had expected. I had terrible problems getting any IBM men to accompany this seventy-two-year-old gentleman on his various tours. During his visit he wanted to see Washington, DC, Wall Street, the Joe Louis fight, the courthouses, football games, the World Series games, and other sites and activities. I even sent him to Chicago to see the stockyards and enjoy the delights of the Windy City, routing him back to New York via Niagara Falls.

I felt sorry for him when, unable to find anyone to take him to see the Yankees and the Dodgers in the World Series, I had to take him to Yankee Stadium myself and explain the game to him. We sat amidst some Dodgers fans who I thought would explode listening to this baseball-ignorant female Yankee fan trying to explain the intricacies and subtleties of baseball. When I finished, Mr. Howard asked in his broad accent, "I say there, who is that behind the wicket?" One of the Dodgers fans took over, and we all became buddies with lots of laughter and rooting for both teams.

Mr. Howard also enjoyed music and theater. In the fall of 1950, he saw everything from "Peter Pan" to "Call Me Madam" to "Guys and Dolls," followed by nightcaps at "21." Jane Haislip or I or any other IBM executive who lived in Manhattan and had nothing to do in the evening would accompany him. What a delight to watch this old gentleman having such a good time at the theater. From the way he spoke, we doubted he ever attended the London theaters while at home.

Although I sometimes felt annoyed when I had to interrupt my real work to escort Mr. Howard to various activities, he seemed so excited and curious about the world around him that the assignment turned out to be one of the more memorable and enjoyable ones I ever had at IBM.

An Expansion of Duties

When Mr. Watson returned from Europe that year, our usual

welcoming committee met him on the pier. And this time his five-year-old granddaughter, Jeannette, Tom and Olive's daughter, joined us. Running up to her grandfather, she asked him when he would take her on a trip.

Mr. Watson asked, "And where would you like to go, my dear?"

"Oh, I want to go to Bethlehem to see where Jesus was born," she replied.

A few weeks later Mr. Watson asked if I would do him a favor by riding up to Endicott on the Erie Railroad. He planned to go up that same day on the Delaware Lackawanna with little Jeannette. When I asked why I couldn't ride on the same train with him and his granddaughter, he said, "I want it to look like she and I are making this trip alone. My secretary will sit in the back of the car in case I need him."

So I canceled a couple of dates and climbed aboard the "weary" Erie so I would be at the Homestead to greet Jeannette and her grandfather, as if I lived there always. As soon as Mr. Watson saw Charlie Kirk, vice president of IBM Manufacturing, the two went into a huddle and stayed there the rest of the evening. That's when I discovered my vice presidential duties had been expanded to include babysitting.

I wanted to retire early, so I suggested we have dinner, play a few games, then she could kiss her grandfather good night. But Jeannette had different ideas. She announced that she always had a bath before going to bed. So into the big seven-foot bathtub she went. I had never bathed a five-year-old before, so I sat on my knees next to the tub hanging on to her tightly for fear she would drown.

As I scrubbed out the huge tub for Grandfather Watson's use later, I laughed myself silly, thinking about my sudden demotion to scrub woman. No wonder he hadn't told me what he wanted me to do in Endicott that weekend. I laughed again when I realized that instead of taking Jeannette to Bethlehem where Jesus was born, Mr. Watson had taken her instead to Painted Post, New York, not far from Endicott, where he was born!

Faith to Move a Mountain

I'm glad to say I wasn't the only one willing to perform unique and surprising assignments for this persuasive man. In June of 1948, additions to the Poughkeepsie IBM plant had been completed and dedication ceremonies planned, with many local VIPs and New York friends invited. The day before the dedication, Mr. Watson, in a final planning session for the big event, decided that the large hill between the plant and the main highway should be removed. It worried him that passersby on the main road into Poughkeepsie couldn't clearly see the huge IBM sign on the new addition because that mammoth mound of earth stood in the way.

"And I want that dirt removed by tomorrow morning at 11 a.m. when the ceremonies begin," declared Mr. Watson as he stared at poor Dause Bibby, the head of our Poughkeepsie plant.

Those of us present at that planning session were struck dumb at the idea of completing such a huge project in a matter of hours. Nobody got much sleep that night for wondering whether those bulldozers with their enormous searchlights would accomplish their mission. But by 11:00 the next morning the hill had disappeared, and none of the guests could have possibly imagined what went on during the preceding twenty hours.

Format Changes

By 1951, the Hundred Percent Club had grown much too large for an Endicott convention. So, each office held its own event, with one of us from World Headquarters as the chief speaker brought in to discuss the latest computer in the works, assure IBMers that we would be vindicated in a lawsuit brought against us by the U.S. government for monopolistic practices, and to congratulate the men and women who made the Club that year and present them with their bonus checks.

The lawsuit, which I had to discuss at each meeting where I spoke, was the U.S. Government's antitrust suit against IBM. Beginning during the Truman administration, the Justice Department had won several antimonopoly cases each year. The government broke Alcoa's hold on the aluminum market, and a few years later forced the United Shoe Machinery Corporation to diversify. Mr. Watson Sr. just knew that sooner or later the government would come after us, and they did. Just because IBM owned ninety percent of the market for punch cards, with little competition, the government considered us a monopoly, but IBM could prove we weren't. (A few years later, IBM finally won their case, after handing over hundreds of documents, dealing with countless investigations, and spending many hours tied up in court proceedings.)

By April of 1951, Headquarters had instructed 181 IBM offices throughout the country to reserve the best available place in each city and to select anything on the menu the honorees would like to eat. From Duluth, Minnesota to Texas, I ate twenty-six consecutive dinners of shrimp cocktail, steak and baked potato, followed by Baked Alaska for dessert. When the executives all returned to New York and exchanged experiences it seemed we each had had the same menu throughout our tours. Mr. Watson remarked, "I think IBM must have cornered the shrimp market all over the country."

The dinner held in San Juan by our Puerto Rico office, however, turned out to be the most unique. They had asked Mr. Watson Sr. to speak, but he refused to fly anywhere in those days, so at the last minute—per usual—he assigned me to go. The IBM manager there had booked the dinner at the new Caribe Hilton hotel on its opening night, and the hotel staff was understandably more concerned with Conrad Hilton's opening dinner party on the roof, than with our paltry group of about twenty-five. So, they set us up on the main floor under the stairs that led to the gambling casino, in an area where the hotel stored extra pianos and other paraphernalia. Consequently, throughout the evening tourists wandered in looking for the casino, and waiters (not ours) dropped by now and then to pick up a piano or extra chairs.

The manager of IBM's San Juan office, a handsome but very nervous man and new to his job, had never conducted a dinner like this before. He had ordered Cornish game hen for the entrée, but when we got our dinners, the hens were still frozen to the bone, and our attempts to cut into them made them fly onto the floor, into our laps, and onto our neighbors' plates. With the dinner in shambles, we tried to inject some humor by making a competition out of it: who could carve his or her bird the best without incident. We had a few words for the captain, too, the nicest of which were that we'd like to have whatever Conrad Hilton was serving upstairs.

To make matters worse, I didn't realize until halfway through my talk that most of my audience didn't speak a word of English. So when it came time to hand out the checks, I lined up the salesmen who had made the Hundred Percent Club and asked their wives to make presentations and reward their husbands with a big kiss. That got them laughing at last.

More Health Issues

On May first of that year I once again entered the hospital, this time to have major surgery for a malignancy, in two operations three days apart. My right lung, still collapsed by pneumo treatments, made for a trickier operation. But I survived the ordeal, and was away from IBM 116 days that summer convalescing once again with my family in California. By the end of summer I returned to World Headquarters. The psychiatrist couch still sat in my office in case I felt tired. I never did. But I did feel terribly obligated to my company for putting up with my operations and keeping me on the payroll.

For awhile I felt depressed about the state of my health and my inability to do much of anything as far as work was concerned. I spoke to Tom, offering to resign from the company, but he wouldn't hear of it. He said I meant too much to the company, and added, "Nor would my father even consider it. So get that out of your head." Of course his reply relieved me, but I felt depressed nevertheless. Tuberculosis is a very debilitating disease and, coupled with a case of cancer, attacked my self-assurance and gave me a grim outlook on life. Tom did his best to bolster my ego, and I felt grateful for his compassion.

"We have the Hundred Percent Club dinners coming up after

the first of the year," he said, "and if you feel well enough to take some of those I sure would appreciate it." I never would have thought those dinners would boost my spirits, but they did.

Jeanne Cotten by now had announced her engagement to be married in January of 1952. Jane Haislip had been promoted to the new IBM World Trade Company, now a subsidiary of the company, as executive assistant to Dick Watson, who now headed World Trade. Mr. Watson Sr. elevated himself to chairman of the board with Mr. Phillips as vice-chairman. And Tom at last became president of IBM; everyone in the company had waited a long time for this well-deserved appointment.

A True Honor

29 October 1951

Dear Miss Leach:

The faculty and Board of Trustees of Mills College have asked me to extend to you their invitation to be present at our commencement exercises on the afternoon of Sunday, 9 June 1952, to receive the honorary degree of doctor of laws. This will be a particularly festive occasion since it marks the centennial of our particular stream of educational tradition which started in 1852 with the founding of the Benicia Female Seminary out of which Mills College emerged...We plan to present honorary degrees to a small group of women who are western either by birth or adoption and who have made significant contributions to their particular fields of endeavor. The fact that you are one of the most distinguished women in American business is made the happier in our slightly provincial minds by the fact that you are an Oaklander as well!

I very much hope that you can arrange to be with us at our centennial commencement, for in honoring you the College would be honoring itself.

Very sincerely yours,
Lynn White Jr., President

What a thrill to receive that letter from Mills College of Oakland, California, inviting me to receive an honorary degree along with nine other native California women who had achieved success in their fields. My friend, Dr. Lillian Gilbreth, the famous engineer of time and motion study and of "Cheaper by the Dozen" fame, gave the commencement address. Agnes de Mille, dance choreographer, Georgia O'Keeffe, artist, San Francisco civic leaders, and others all received honorary degrees.

President White read my citation as follows: "Thoughtful feminine invader of the masculine realm whose motto is THINK, unmechanized mind presiding over mechanical brains, the degree of DOCTOR OF LAWS HONORIS CAUSA..." Dr. White wasn't as kind to Mrs. Gilbreth, who had given birth to twelve children. He introduced her to the audience that day as "the biological phenomenon of this century." Still, I felt honored to have been included in this very select group, particularly when they never asked for a contribution of any kind from IBM. All the other institutions that had honored me over the years had. So I cherished this recognition most of all.

Food for Thought (Or Just for Attendance)

After every IBM stockholders meeting, all of which were held in the showroom on the main floor of World Headquarters, the company presented a beautifully catered luncheon, held on the second floor. I always thought the only female corporate vice president should escort the few female stockholders upstairs to lunch following the meeting.

On one occasion, two elderly ladies from New Jersey sat alone among a sea of men in the audience. They looked so uncomfortable and out of place, I knew they must have inherited their stock from their husbands. Obviously they had never been to an IBM meeting before and were delighted by the special treatment. I sat them down on either side of me and tried to draw them into a conversation, but they simply couldn't talk, probably, I thought, frightened by this new experience of attending the annual meeting of a big company. When the main course of delicious roast beef arrived, the woman on my left leaned across to her friend on my right and said, "Mabel, this is much better than Westinghouse, isn't it?" I had difficulty keeping a straight face. I could just see these two going from one annual meeting to another, not to learn anything but to eat, and I realized I was sitting right in the middle of a New Yorker cartoon. Later, I related this incident to Mr. Watson, and I'd never heard him laugh so hard as he did then.

CHAPTER TWENTY

New Journeys—To IBM's Europe and Beyond

In the spring of 1953, Jane Haislip and I once again planned a trip to Europe. We'd planned a similar trip in 1951 but my surgery pre-empted that summer vacation. In early April, Tom Jr. called us both from Endicott to say that in July, he wanted us to serve as delegates to the International Organization of Business and Professional Women conference in Stockholm. He added, "When Dad gets back to New York City he will want to review with you the itinerary he'd like you to follow."

Imagine our surprise and complete delight at this phone call. Traveling in Europe on IBM time meant doors would be opened to us which otherwise would not, and some with red carpets behind them, too. We would see places and meet people we otherwise would not, though we would have to forego some of the places we planned to visit on our own. We could hardly wait for our meeting with Mr. Watson to find out how this assignment came about.

I scheduled my annual checkup with my doctors, and I looked forward to putting that behind me. The X-rays, however, looked grim, and I thought this might doom me to miss another beautifully planned trip to Europe because of an operation. This time, Tom Jr. urged me to have the surgery at the Sloan-Kettering Cancer Hospital in New York where he served on the board. I agreed, with full confidence that no more malignancy would be discovered. Thank heavens, I was right. The culprits turned out to be adhesions from the previous operations, and my surgeon, Dr. Brunschwig, assured me I could attend the big meeting in Stockholm in July providing I rested for a month afterward.

Jane sailed with the Watson party in June, and I flew to Stockholm ten days later in time for the opening of the conference, holding my incision together, but with my surgeon's blessing. He too planned to be in Copenhagen for a medical meeting, so I could see him there for further check- ups.

The meeting in Stockholm impressed us, indeed, showcasing several women in their native dress. I still wasn't used to separating the ewes from the rams, which was why I had resigned from the Business and Professional Women's Club. I never had time to go to their meetings, although I had served as a principal speaker at several of their programs. And now here I sat, attending their international meeting as a delegate.

The European women seemed primarily professional women while the American members were mostly businesswomen. The program was dedicated to the betterment of women at the workplace, and we heard some beautifully expressed speeches. We also enjoyed the elaborate formal dinner on our final night held in the handsome town hall of Stockholm with its gilt walls and golden dinner service.

Mr. Watson instructed Jane and me to give a luncheon for the American Business and Professional Club women, which we did in the Grand Hotel ballroom. We placed favors of Swedish hand-carved, small horses at each place as mementos from Mr. Watson of the Stockholm conference. Shopping for these and preparing a speech for the occasion knocked me out for the next day and a half, but the U.S. delegation really appreciated the luncheon.

The purpose of our trip to IBM's European offices was to inspect and update all educational material used in each country. We started in Stockholm, then traveled to Oslo, and finally Copenhagen, where I chose to spend my month of rest and check in with Dr. Brunschwig. Besides, I had a couple of friends there, in case I needed any. Jane proceeded on to Germany and Switzerland alone, then to Italy. We joined forces again in Paris, where the Watsons and their party also spent the week. Jane and I went on to Brussels by train and then to Amsterdam, chauffeured in the European IBM manager's limousine. During our stay, IBM dedicated a new IBM plant in Amsterdam, so we attended the ceremony. We flew to London for a week of inspecting and updating, then sailed from Southhampton on the Ile de France, reaching New York about eight weeks after we'd left.

If our hearts weren't quite as young and gay as Cornelia Otis Skinner's and Emily Kimbrough's, we did have our share of funny adventures. We even met two queens along the way—sort of. The first was Queen Louise of Sweden, who invited all the ladies from the conference to visit Drottningholm, her beautiful summer palace in the country. Although we stood in the same room with her we didn't see her standing in her pink gown on a pink rug against a pink wall. Against the opposite wall stood all her cabinet members lined up in their morning coats. As we walked by and greeted each of them, thinking the queen was probably standing at the end of the queue somewhere, she stood watching the backs of our heads as we passed by. Jane and I had instructions to shake her hand and give her a message from Mr. Watson, but we missed our chance. We swore we wouldn't tell him; we felt like such fools, and she was his favorite queen!

More Royalty

While visiting my Danish friends, Alix and Ivar Vind, whom I had met in New York years before, I got to meet Queen Ingrid of Denmark, who came to call for the purpose of presenting to Alix a lovely diamond and sapphire pin from the Queen Mother, who had recently died. I had known Alix for years, but I never knew until that moment that she was the niece of King Frederick of Denmark. Queen Ingrid (the daughter of the King of Sweden) brought along her three little girls and their governess, Mary North, plus her best friend from Stockholm who was visiting her at the time. I could hardly wait to tell Mr. Watson that I had tea with a queen he had never met!

Since the Danes dislike pomp and ceremony, Queen Ingrid wished to make her presentation to Alix and Ivar in private. So the rest of us, including the three little princesses, went out in the garden to play. There I sat playing "London Bridge" with Margrethe, the present Queen of Denmark, and her sisters. Mary North, whose father had been an admiral in the British navy, had just returned from the coronation of Queen Elizabeth of England at Westminster Abbey, and had many stories to tell. Queen Ingrid, knowing of the close friendship between the Vinds and Mary, insisted Mary stay for dinner with us, saying she (the Queen) would love to be alone with her children and tuck them into bed herself for a change.

What a great treat for this American to hear Mary's version of the coronation: who attended, and how many people were related to the Danish royal family. I felt like a fly on the wall of Westminster Abbey that night.

Hush Hush

The State Department had informed Jane and me before we left that no IBMer should mention the newest computer (the 701) while abroad, particularly in Europe, nor discuss it with IBM personnel in Europe, even though *LIFE* magazine had carried a two-page spread on this latest IBM machine the week I left. Everyone we encountered in IBM Europe, of course, wanted to know the latest, but we had to follow orders and play dumb. This proved terribly embarrassing, particularly at a time when IBM was still working to build foreign confidence. And what kind of confidence could the Europeans have in Jane and me as IBM's apparently ignorant representatives? But those were our orders.

At the same time we were in Europe, Senator Joe McCarthy's attorney and advisor, Roy Cohn and a Mr. Schine, were also there collecting information for the senator. Jane and I, who hadn't heard of them before, constantly met with questions about these two that we couldn't answer. What did America think of them? Why were they poking around Europe? The International Herald Tribune didn't tell us, so we merely dismissed their "investigations" as a political ploy to bring notoriety to the senator. We hadn't read an American newspaper for some time and knew nothing about Senator McCarthy's antics in Congress. But in Paris we learned of his vicious attacks on the State Department to rid itself of the alleged two hundred communists employed there. Later, he conducted hearings against the United States Army, which brought him notoriety, much criticism and created a furor in our government. His bitter attacks of abuse and insults on his fellow members of the Senate finally were condemned, bringing an end to the political life of Senator McCarthy.

Love and Art

During my so-called "vacation of rest" in Copenhagen, I did a lot of thinking about my future, my obligation to IBM, my health problems, and my personal life. In March of 1953, I had met Bill Pollock, president of his family's company in Chestnut Hill, Pennsylvania. He had been very attentive to me during that year's operation and had shown particular kindness to my mother, who had flown East to take care of me. When I finally felt able to fly to Europe he didn't want me to go, but I felt obligated to join Jane on this mission. Sitting and musing for a month in Copenhagen, I realized I loved him.

When I didn't see him at the pier on our return to New York, my heart sank. But I soon discovered that his 90-year-old widowed father had died that morning, and his sister, who had just given birth to her first child, had returned to the family home to convalesce. No wonder he didn't meet me at the pier.

Bill continued to court me as I tackled a new assignment: evaluating IBM's Fine Arts Department. In the late '30s, IBM hired a remarkable lady, Marinobel Smith, to build an art collection for the company, starting with the 79 paintings from the 79 countries where we did business. These paintings hung in the IBM exhibits at the 1939 World Fairs in New York and San Francisco.

The following year at both fairs, IBM displayed a collection of art from each state of the United States, including pieces of sculpture from each state. We bought part of a famous collection of miniature rooms, known then as Mrs. Thorne's Miniatures, which became another part of the IBM touring collection of art. Also, a fabulous collection of wooden replicas of Leonardo da Vinci's inventions carved by an Italian artist became very popular on the IBM art tour of colleges and universities in Europe and the U.S. All in all, Marinobel Smith organized twenty-nine various exhibits for tour in the U.S., Europe, and even behind the Iron Curtain.

On one of Marinobel's buying tours to South America, she acquired native costumes from each country, sometimes buying them right off people's backs. These, together with the flags of each country, were constantly in use by various organizations, including the United Nations, and were veritable public relations treasures. The lively department of IBM in charge of all these artifacts became my responsibility when Marinobel had to leave New York because of health reasons.

In addition to the IBM collections we had touring Europe and the U.S., and all the paintings hung in the offices at World Headquarters and various IBM plants, the company had 450 paintings housed in crates in a New York City warehouse, some of which had never been opened. I had to evaluate these and dispose of, or hang them in the company's country clubs and executive offices.

Recognizing my own limits as an art critic, I asked Mr. James Barrie, head of Grand Central Art Galleries, to help me in this task. We watched with great interest the reactions of the men at Hahn's warehouse, where these paintings were stored, as they uncrated them. These men were really our best, most experienced judges since they were exposed to so much art of the city stored there, and with their help we kept the best paintings and sent the others on to be sold.

We still had some Hundred Percent Club dinners to organize before the end of the year, and Tom Jr. asked me to handle them. After one dinner near Chicago, I sneaked a quick trip to San Francisco so I could introduce Bill Pollock to my family and show him the place where I was born and raised. During that whirlwind four-day visit, I finally made my decision to resign at the end of December and get married.

By mid-1953, with Tom at the helm, IBM had become almost completely computerized, with the 701 now in the limelight. A new technology had taken over while I had stayed busy in the public relations field or having an operation, so I was no longer involved in the mainstream projects. Tom Jr. had his own inner circle of computer experts and executives to help him direct the company's future, just as his father had had his own advisors, a circle I'd been part of. But, understandably, I didn't fit into Tom's group, although he continued to give me assignments he knew I could handle.

I'd traveled some rough roads during my IBM career. Now, my lung had come back up fairly well after eight long years of pneumothorax treatment and three major operations, and I felt ready for another kind of life, but not necessarily a technological one.

IBM had treated me well, awarding me various promotions, giving me many opportunities to grow with each assignment, and allowing me to represent all the women of the company. For that reason, I found it difficult to say farewell to the only company I'd ever known. I will always feel grateful to the entire Watson family for their compassion and consideration during all my illnesses. I loved meeting all the famous people who inspired me along the way, but most of all I cherished the deep friendships I made with my fellow IBMers. The bond we forged among us has lasted all these years.

To my knowledge, no one has ever given enough credit to the systems service women who worked so diligently for IBM during World War II. They were the ones who helped me over fifty years ago to become Big Blue's pioneer woman, and I still salute them.

EPILOGUE

Thank heavens for all the wonderful advice, training, and amazing experiences I had during my IBM years. Without them I would never have developed in mind, body and spirit into the resilient person I needed to be to help me face the challenges I've had through the years.

Forty-six years ago, in January of 1954, I married Bill Pollock. He immediately decided we should live in the country, twenty-five miles outside of Philadelphia in the beautiful rolling hills of Pennsylvania Dutch Country. We put down roots there, attending church, and joining in the community. I was so used to being busy that I volunteered for as many projects as I could, including teaching Sunday school and needlepointing church cushions 'til my fingers ached.

During that time, I decided to enroll in the Ambler School of Horticulture. Before long I found myself a member of the Pennsylvania Horticultural Society, which puts on the Pennsylvania Flower Show. This was, and still is, the largest flower show in the country, and I enjoyed being involved with it. In fact, I enjoyed my work with the society so much that I was invited by a well-known horticulturist of the day, Ernesta Ballard, executive director of the society, to become a member of the board. My board duties brought me into contact with many interesting people, including Atlee Burpee, of Burpee Seed fame, and another horticulturist who had just returned from decorating the White House for Tricia Nixon Cox's wedding.

All that activity came to a sudden stop when there arrived on our doorstep the loveliest little girl, Elizabeth Leach Pollock, seven days old. She brought us such joy and happiness through those years. We made several trips to the West Coast and to Michigan to introduce her to cousins, aunts, uncles and grandparents. Then, when Betsy turned ten, we made the first of many trips to Europe, so she could meet her other aunts, uncles and cousins.

During those years, I suffered horribly from allergies, especially during ragweed season. So, each year during the worst time, we rented a house on the West Coast. In 1969, my allergies became so severe that we decided to move. We spent two years living in Lausanne, Switzerland. Then we returned and made our home in Pebble Beach, California.

Once again I threw myself into volunteer work, which I have continued since then. I served on the board of the United Way of Monterey Peninsula, the Board of Trustees of Monterey Institute of International Studies (four years as its chairperson), and the board of the Del Monte Forest Foundation (1980-1986).
Bill, in ailing health, passed away in 1977, on our daughter's 21st birthday. In 1983, after seven years of widowhood, I re-met Wilbur K. Amonette, whom I had not seen since college, 40 years before. We had much in common; not only were we both graduates of the University of California, Berkeley, but like me, K started with IBM at the World's Fair in San Francisco. He was a widower, retired after thirty-five years with IBM.

Following his retirement, K was invited to join other former top business executives as part of a New York City partnership created to solve some of the problems of that city, such as a need for better schools and more low-cost housing. He never intended to continue in this partnership for long, and after five years decided he'd had enough, and he and his wife moved back to the West Coast to be near family and friends. She died shortly after they made the move. I married K in October 1983 and we have enjoyed sixteen years of joy, happiness, and lots of travel.

I've received numerous awards over the years, some of which I mentioned earlier in the book. In 1988, the Chancellor of the University of California, Berkeley, appointed me a "Berkeley Fellow," a designation I felt proud to bear. And in 1996, I was inducted into the Women In Technology International Hall of Fame. Since I couldn't attend the ceremony to pick up my plaque, IBM actually sent a video crew to my home to tape my acceptance speech, which was then shown to those attending the induction ceremony.

So here I am, a lively, "young" eighty-two-year-old about to face the biggest challenge of my life. Not long ago, as the result of a rare medical condition, I lost sight in both eyes. I'm now having to relearn how to eat, how to walk, how to dress myself, virtually how to do everything. It's been a real learning experience, but as we used to say at IBM:

"The difficult we do at once,
the impossible takes a little longer."

Me and my husband K Amonette.